I THINK I CAN

William Breisky

I THINK I CAN

1974

DOUBLEDAY & COMPANY, INC.
GARDEN CITY, NEW YORK

Library of Congress Cataloging in Publication Data
Breisky, William.
    I think I can.
    1. Brain-damaged children—Personal narratives.
2. Breisky, Karen Luise, 1965–   I. Title.
RJ486.B69   362.7′8′30924 [B]
Library of Congress Catalog Card Number 73–15326

Portion from *Joe Egg* reprinted by permission of Grove Press, Inc.,
copyright © 1967 by Peter Nichols, and by permission of Faber and
Faber Ltd.

To KAREN, of course,

for reshaping our priorities and our definitions of love and spirit and achievement. But also to John and Gretchen, who contributed challenge and joy . . . to the man in the red Ford . . . to Dolly Bean, who assured us of Karen's "submerged intelligence" . . . to Billy Kirchmeier, who knew Karen would walk again . . . to Lyne Genereux, who invited Karen to pull her zipper . . . to Glenn Doman, whom Karen hopes to marry one day . . . to Sally and Ralph, who make the City of Brotherly Love a reality . . . to all those people who have worked to make a difference in Karen's life and who may or may not be mentioned on these pages . . . and especially to Karen's mother and grandmother, who have taught Karen to do her best.

Contents

I THINK I CAN

CHAPTER I

Last Sunday

I cannot write of tomorrow—yet I know Karen will contribute something significant to it.

I cannot say how things might have gone with another child—for we've seen others, hurt less cruelly than Karen, who struggled hard yet still lie helpless.

I can only state with assurance that our Karen, who suffered massive brain injury at the age of two, and seemed lost, fought her way back and has taught us much.

This will be, essentially, a story of a human spirit—of some well of strength within Karen—and it is difficult to pinpoint the moment in time when such a story should logically begin or end. I suppose it begins on whatever day it was that Karen took a look at the world around her and determined she would like to be a part of things. And her story will not end until that day when all those who have been touched by her spirit are gone.

Because last Sunday—the day this book began—was a day when past and present seemed to meet, I'll begin by telling how it was then with us—John, Karen, Gretchen, Barbara, Doc and myself—at Eastleigh, our sixty-year-old, white-roofed, rented Bermuda home.

The girls had a strawberry-yogurt bonus for their Sunday breakfast. At five, Gretchen rates cheese fondue her favorite dish. Karen, at seven, is especially partial to roast beef, cucumber slices, and Bermuda-grown carrots. But yogurt—any flavor, any time—rates high on both their lists of good things to eat, so they approached their Sunday breakfast bonus with enthusiasm.

Suddenly Gretchen had an inspired idea. "Let's eat this like we eat spaghetti, Karen," she said, and with typical dexterity she commenced twisting her spoon in the yogurt dish, much as she twists a fork in her spaghetti.

Karen thought the game a splendid one, but her fingers couldn't quite co-operate, and soon half of her first spoonful was decorating the tablecloth.

Gretchen said the obvious. "Oh, Karen—you spilled some!"

"Well," Karen retorted, laughing delightedly, "that's how I eat spaghetti!"

Karen's sense of humor had come to the rescue once again, and I made a mental note to record the spaghetti story in one of the small notebooks that Karen refers to collectively as "my book." Then I begged everyone's indulgence. I said I would like to sit under the Bermuda sun for an hour or so, with my notebooks, to think about converting "my book" into a book for the rest of the world.

But as I surveyed the flat-calm waters of Bermuda's Great Sound—a shimmering plain of blue, below and beyond the bananas and oleanders that fringe the grounds of Eastleigh— I decided that, before reviewing the past, I should take an inventory of "today." A ruled pad of paper attached to a clipboard became my inventory book.

John. Began life as the largest infant in a large maternity ward, and at the age of nine is almost as strong as his mother. Sandy-haired, engaging, competitive. Patient when he's standing on Flat Rock with a fishing line, impatient when he's involved in a project and things aren't going his way. Hard of hearing when he is reading a Hardy Boys adventure or when advised that he had better get on with his chores if he expects to collect his allowance. Capable of preparing a first-rate breakfast for himself and his sisters, but not yet capable of recalling when last he polished his school shoes.

Karen. Imaginative, loving, determined. An imp for her first

two years, a worker for the past five (but still part imp).
Handicapped in countless ways, superior in others. One of the
world's great listeners. The least fussy eater in the family.
(During her long period of sightlessness she rejected food
only on grounds of bad taste or smell—never because "it looks
yucky.") Unable to button buttons, but invariably able to get
to the heart of the matter with an appropriate punch line.

Gretchen. A born mimic. Bright and bug-eyed. Answers to
"Grouchen," but in fact asks little more of life than a supply
of paper and a crayon or felt-tip pen. Nearing her sixth birthday, she's responsible for keeping flowers on the dining table
and for assuring that her brother and sister don't receive more
than their share of the batch of cookies just removed from the
oven.

Barbara. The family's baker of cookies, as well as our arts
and crafts instructor, pet-care expert, costume designer, chor-
eographer, repairer of bruised knees and feelings, gardener. Dark
of hair and light of feet. Somehow amalgamates her father's
temper and her mother's patience. Rebels against a programmed
way of life—and yet has devoted herself to a relentless, hour-
after-hour, day-after-day, year-after-year program of activities that
has brought Karen back.

Doktor Pfeffer of the cold, wet nose. Better known as Doc.
Eleven-year-old noisy schnauzer, faithful friend. Formerly listed
on the masthead of our New England newspaper as Office
Dog. Has nipped our postman's leg because he distrusts uniforms, and John's cheek because John fell on him after leaning
back too far on his chair at the dinner table. Stands sentinel
over the proceedings whenever Karen "does a program."

With my cast of characters assembled, I began my inventory
of assorted props and sets:

A blue-tailed lizard, I noted in my inventory book, is perched
on the hank of near-ripe bananas cut yesterday and now taking
the sun alongside the doorstep outside our kitchen door.

Ernie and Bert, Karen's pet guinea pigs, are whistling a
happy tune in their backyard playpen.

"Moses in the Bullrushes," inspired by John when he was two and sculpted by our incomparable friend Fingal Rosenquist, reclines at the top of the stairway, alongside the sandals left behind by Karen's friend Lee Ann.

Blue swim fins are drying in the sun on the patio behind the kitchen.

Morning glory vines outside our bedroom window climb thirty feet to cloak the graying branches of a dead Bermuda cedar.

The upstairs doorknobs hold their quota of belts and pajama tops.

The downstairs playroom—once a neighborhood grocery—is a gymnasium on holiday. Its wall lined with apparatus built and installed for "Karen's program," it sits idle much of the time now, while Karen practices "just being a kid."

And the walls tell our life story: portraits of my Austrian great-grandfather and his wife—he in the uniform of the emperor's horse cavalry—passed on to me, the eldest son, after my parents had died; John's framed and mounted seashell collection; Grandfather Baer's sketch of a hollyhock patch in East Orange, New Jersey; the lion mask Barbara made for a school play last year; the slightly erotic temple rubbing Aunt Clara brought back from Thailand two years ago; an old print of the city of Carlisle, given Barbara when the art gallery that employed her as a bachelor girl went out of business; a wooden Dutch cookie press sent us by brother Arthur and sister-in-law Marlene from The Hague; John's prize-winning Bermuda kite; a boldly splashed watercolor landscape by Gretchen, taped to the broom closet door; and in a place of honor over the sofa, the Cornwall scene we bought in the village of Chagford, on the fringe of Dartmoor.

My inventory-taking is interrupted by Karen's announcement that there will be a "porch lunch" today and that she would appreciate some help in picking flowers for the lunch table.

"Come down along the road with me, Daddy. I went hunting along the drive and couldn't find things that looked nice. When I found one flower and gave it to my Lefty, the orange

and red petals fell off and just the green stem was left."
("Lefty" is Karen's stubborn left hand, which refuses to turn
palm up and can't be of much help when it comes to picking
flowers, but can at least hold flowers for "Righty.")

"You're really in a flower-picking mood, aren't you, Karen?"

"Yes! Because I like flowers, and because I want to write
Käthe and tell her that sometimes *I* pick flowers, too."

(Käthe Kirchmeier, aged twenty, of Enfield, Connecticut,
has been Karen's constant pal and prodder in the lifetime since
Karen's brain was hurt, in 1967. It was Käthe who enthusiasti-
cally joined us in urging Karen to emulate the Little Blue
Engine—"I *think* I can, I *think* I can"—when Karen was struggling to learn creeping and knee-walking, and now a recent
letter of Käthe's that said, "Gretchen, have you been keeping
the table supplied with flowers?" was inspiring Karen to have
a go at flower arranging.)

Four hibiscus blossoms grace the table at Sunday lunchtime.
John's buddies Martin and Michael, sons of a Welsh neighbor, join us for grilled-cheese sandwiches. Martin says he's
never had a grilled-cheese sandwich before.

John, Martin and Michael—promptly joined by five other
boys—retire to John's tree house after lunch, and Barbara ar-
ranges to deliver Karen to Lee Ann's.

It takes a bit of planning to help Karen "just be a kid."
After more than five years of being "programmed" daily—on
the floor, on a "patterning table," on slides and ladders, even
in a darkened closet—Karen is to be given a period of freedom.
The major obstacles have been hurdled; now, the experts theo-
rize, the example and company of other children might be
stimulus enough to move her forward. But this means a period
of adjustment for all of us. We must try not to feel guilty when
free moments are not devoted to Karen's program, and we must
arrange more visits for Karen to the homes of friends, such as
Lee Ann.

When Barbara and the girls reach the bottom of the driveway and turn in the direction of Lee Ann's house, I invite

Doktor Pfeffer of the cold, wet nose to visit our special corner of the Great Sound with me.

On the homemade concrete platform amid coral outcroppings we fondly refer to as "our waterfront," Doc contemplates the incoming tide, sniffs at crevices, cautiously explores a pool of ankle-deep water, and when I remove his leash, he traces a happy circle in the air with his nose and wags his entire body.

Waves of "waterfront" memories come in. John's first, excited encounter with an octopus. Our introduction to snorkeling, tracking the route of a conch who has made his ponderously slow way along the sandy bottom. Gail Ellis, who had organized our teams of "patterning ladies" back in Connecticut, organizing John, Karen and Gretchen for their first proper swimming lesson. Karen, buoyed by water wings but her legs churning in the warm water: "Daddy, look at me!"

Two tourists stop to photograph one another posing in the moongate at the head of our cove, and this intrusion of the present somehow makes the sounds of Sunday afternoon more insistent: a kiskadee gives a sharp cry as he alights on a casuarina limb; two blasts of her horn announce that a Swedish cruise ship is hoisting anchor and preparing to steam out of Grassy Bay; a Honda and a Kawasaki challenge the island's twenty-mile-per-hour speed limit on our open stretch of Sound View Road; a shrill "C'mon—hit it!" resounds from our lawn, where John and his mates are punching a beach ball back and forth over the badminton net.

I resnap Doc's leash, walk up to the road, sit on the limestone-block wall the children and I like to inspect with flashlights on summer evening tree-frog hunts. A sudden tug on Doc's leash calls my attention to the fact that "Taffy"—Yorkshire terrier, female—is heading in our direction. At the other end of Taffy's leash is Wes Lewis—Canadian Navy, father of our children's chums Scott, Todd and Lynn.

Wes takes a seat on the wall, two leash-lengths away, in the late afternoon sun, and we speak of lobster diving, of boy upbringing, and of schnauzers versus yorkies. I tell Wes of

Karen's "be a kid" prescription, and he recalls the afternoon, this past summer, when our girls were given permission for the first time to walk up the road to the Lewis house.

At the foot of our drive, Gretchen had taken Karen's hand and they had sung an exuberant "Good-by!" in unison.

"You should have seen Karen's face when she got to our house," Wes recalls. "She was so proud to have made that trip without you or Barbara—it was just as if you'd given her a gallon of her favorite ice cream. And when it was time to go, I said, 'Are you sure you don't want me to take you girls back?' and Karen said, 'No way!' "

Last Sunday ended quietly. John grappled with a French assignment. The girls talked their father into reading an extra chapter of *Charlie and the Chocolate Factory.* And Barbara wrote her weekly summary of events to her parents, now retired in Florida:

> . . . Gretchen's teacher told her she was going to be an artist, so she draws nonstop from morn to night. Every once in a while she shows genius, just a little, but then goes back to pretty ordinary kid stuff.
>
> John is really working hard at school. He enjoys doing well and being ahead of his class—now is doing a math workbook that is quite tough. Glad his teacher isn't afraid to challenge him.
>
> Bill seems to have started on Karen's book. He has started walking around the house with that "somewhere else" look, and a clipboard and pencil in one hand, chewing his knuckle madly. Says he accomplished a lot today.

And I did. At the day's start there had remained the lingering doubt that it was perhaps too soon to write Karen's story—"too soon to crow," as Barbara put it. But somehow this lazy Sunday had dissolved that doubt.

Karen is not yet able to skip rope or ride the bike we gave her for her seventh birthday or bowl a cricket ball through the guest-room window as easily as her brother—or even button her buttons or tie her shoelaces or pull her chair up to the table or look toward the sun. But once she was blind, and now she can read. Once she was speechless, and now she can sing. Once she was immobile, and now she can take her sister's hand and walk up the road to Lynn Lewis's house. Once, locked in a secret world, she had rages of frustration, and now, "I like everybody in my school."

It *is* time to crow.

CHAPTER II

Another Sunday, Long Ago

Karen Luise Breisky was one of seventeen babies delivered at Hartford Hospital on April 27, 1965. Her arrival rated only two lines in the Hartford *Courant,* but at the Thompsonville (Connecticut) *Press,* edited and published by Karen's father, the event was regarded as very important news indeed. Not only had John's baby sister weighed in at an imposing nine pounds eleven ounces, but she had shown exceeding good judgment by arriving late on a Wednesday afternoon, so that her father's weekly newspaper, published every Thursday, would not be scooped on the blessed event by the Hartford and Springfield dailies.

Unfortunately, I muffed the story. I wrote what I considered to be a hilarious column entitled "Only a Girl," in which I said in a studiously offhanded way that I had become the father of a mere daughter, who could never be expected to pitch for the Pirates of my hometown of Pittsburgh or accompany me on fishing trips. The column was misunderstood by at least 52 per cent of our audience—or every female reader.

We brought Karen home to our apartment over the *Press,* where she was promptly adopted by her brother John, then twenty-two months, and by the entire *Press* staff. It had always been Barbara's custom to bring a pot of coffee and a tray of doughnuts downstairs to the news desks and the printing plant on press nights, while the final stories were being set and the final pages locked up, and for the month or two following her arrival baby Karen came along with the refreshments for her ten o'clock feeding.

According to Karen's baby book, she turned herself over at two months, registered her first laugh (inspired by John) at three months, began to creep at seven months, displayed two bottom teeth in a single week at seven and a half months, and stood in her crib at eight months.

By the time baby sister Gretchen decided to be born—on Halloween night, 1966—we were living in a rambling, creaking, marvelous old Federal house a few miles from the *Press*. I recall that Halloween vividly—John pleading to go trick-or-treating, Karen running to the front door to be *presented* candy by a father-and-son team going the rounds in clown suits, Barbara coolly stirring a pot of chili for company and timing her contractions while Gretchen stirred within her.

Barbara, in the years that were to follow, wept often—not wanting to, but unable to suppress the grief—at her mental picture of Karen in the early spring of 1967, exploring the field behind our house with John and stuffing wild flowers in the pocket of her red snowsuit jacket.

Karen could operate John's record player then, and a scratchy 45 called "I Am a Truck" was her absolute favorite.

Karen's first regular "chore" was to scamper up the stairs and to the back of our house, to rap on the door of the cubicle known as "Daddy's office" and announce, "Dinner's ready, Daddy!" When Karen was first given this task, the announcement was run together into a single word—"Du-why-dye!"—but her diction had improved considerably by the time of her second birthday, in April 1967.

On May 12, 1967, according to a slip of yellow paper I tucked away in a desk drawer at the time, and discovered recently, Karen danced triumphantly around our rambling old house, shouting, "*John's* not pretty! John's *not* pretty!"

Recollections of Karen before the night of May 21–22, 1967, are, for me at least, very dim indeed. Something (a blind spot? . . . mixed feelings of pain, guilt, remorse? . . . a subconscious determination not to look backward?) washed out

most of my memories of "the old Karen" very shortly after
she was stricken.

We hadn't really given the matter much thought at the
time, but we later realized that until the night of Sunday,
May 21, we had never had a sick child, had never consulted
our pediatrician for anything other than routine checkups and
shots. So we weren't quite prepared to cope with the trouble
that lay ahead of us.

That long-ago Sunday began quietly enough. We were expecting the Elis Johansons for lunch. We had sipped uncounted
cups of Swedish *glögg* at the Johansons on New Year's Eve,
and now, as they were on the eve of departing for Elis's new
assignment at Iceland's Keflavík airport, we were saying good-by.

Karen's luncheon behavior was not outstanding. Barbara
observed that the beginnings of an apparent cold had made
her cranky, but I didn't notice anything amiss until dessert
time, when Karen, who ordinarily spurned parental help, insisted on sitting in my lap and having me spoon-feed her
vanilla ice cream. She took a nap on a downstairs daybed after
lunch. By evening she was slightly feverish. Barbara gave her a
dose of baby aspirin, put her to bed early, and assured her
that she would feel better in the morning.

Baby Gretchen chose that night to do some serious, nonstop
teething and yowling. Karen was unusually restless. Barbara
said she would go into the front room with Gretch, and I took
Karen into our big bed so that I could hear her. As the night
wore on, Karen's breathing became somewhat labored. I discovered that she was much more comfortable in a semi-sitting
position, propped up against pillows. I spoke to Barbara at some
time during the night and said I thought we should call our
pediatrician as soon as his office opened in the morning.

By half-past five in the morning, Karen's breathing was so
labored that we decided to phone for advice right then. But
our pediatrician operated as one third of a group practice, and
instead of getting him on the phone we got an answering
service, which relayed our call to the "duty doctor." Barbara

detailed the symptoms, even holding Karen to the phone so the doctor could hear her.

"Croup" was his telephone diagnosis. He asked if we had a shower.

Yes.

Fine, he declared. Then take Karen into the bathroom, turn on the hot water full blast, raise some steam, keep her there for twenty minutes or so, and see if that eases her breathing; then give her a warm drink, put her to bed if she's comfortable, and bring her in after the office opens.

I took Karen into our downstairs bathroom and followed the doctor's instructions. The room filled with steam, and after some twenty minutes Karen seemed to be breathing much more easily. Both Karen and I were drenched, so I carried her upstairs to Barbara, then returned to the downstairs bath to shave and clean up.

Barbara dried Karen, dressed her in fresh pajamas, and put her in her crib. Karen seemed comfortable and fell asleep almost immediately. Barbara dressed (she remembers every item of clothing she wore that day) and sat by Karen's crib.

In less than ten minutes Karen suddenly awoke and sat upright. She looked as if she were going to be sick. Barbara took her to the bathroom, where she threw up. The discharge appeared to contain traces of blood.

John, awakened by the commotion, stood outside the bathroom door, wide-eyed and alarmed.

"Run downstairs and get Daddy!" Barbara pleaded. John ran, and returned to report, "Daddy's in the shower." He was sent once again to summon me, and this time he succeeded. I rushed upstairs, where Barbara asked me to phone the doctor. I dialed the doctor's number and left word with his answering service, then phoned the Enfield Police Department and asked them to dispatch the community ambulance to take Karen to the hospital. The desk sergeant said the best they could do was a police cruiser with emergency equipment, but that it would be more than adequate.

While we were waiting for the doctor to return our call, Karen suddenly stiffened and turned bluish. I stood helpless, but Barbara sensed immediately what had to be done. She gave Karen the "kiss of life," breathing air into her lungs, and as our daughter began to gulp mouthfuls of air again for herself, her body relaxed.

The phone rang at that point, and the doctor told us to take Karen to the emergency entrance at Hartford's St. Francis Hospital. He said he would meet us there and that he would phone ahead to assure that the emergency team was ready for us.

While we spoke, a blue police cruiser pulled into our driveway. At the wheel was a veteran police officer, a bear of a man named Nicholas Bartolotta.

Barbara wanted to go with Karen to the hospital. I said I would get a neighbor to look after John and Gretchen, and follow as soon as I could.

Barbara and Karen got into the front seat of the cruiser beside the police officer; an oxygen mask was fitted over Karen's face, and she was wrapped in her pink quilt. I watched and prayed as the cruiser sped south on Enfield Street.

It was about six-thirty when I phoned Mrs. Tom Barbour at the Congregational parsonage across the street. Tom Barbour had been a prime mover in the town's ecumenical movement, and had been fatally stricken with a heart attack a few months previous, while preparing to preach the town's first ecumenical service. The Barbours were people of action. Gwen Barbour, Tom's widow, still living in the parsonage, said she would get dressed and come right over.

I remember telling John not to worry, telling Gwen where things were, trying to be calm, searching for Karen's new white Easter bunny and a few things Barbara might need. I remember having to stop for directions to St. Francis. And I remember the indescribable chill I felt when I found Barbara in the emergency ward, and she told me that Karen had come as near to death as one could come, but now was breathing again.

Barbara and Karen's trip to the hospital had been a night-mare. Encountering bumper-to-bumper traffic on Interstate 91, as first-shift United Aircraft workers headed for their jobs, Nicky Bartolotta had been unable to make good time, even traveling on the shoulder of the highway, so as he approached Windsor he decided to exit onto the old Route 5A for the final few miles to Hartford.

The police siren was wailing as the cruiser sped through Windsor—but not loudly enough. Nicky Bartolotta applied his brakes but could not avoid plowing into the car that crossed his path at an intersection. The other car spun around, ejecting the driver.

No one was seriously hurt, but both cars were put out of commission and precious moments were ticking away. As Officer Bartolotta radioed for help, Barbara pleaded with him to flag down another car. He stopped a sedan with two elderly people in it. Barbara, frantic, could see them converse briefly; then the car drove on.

A young man who contributed as much as anyone to the saving of Karen's life was delivered to us a moment later. He wore the clothes of a factory worker. He drove a red hardtop—a Ford, Barbara thinks. And he drove like a man possessed, flooring the accelerator, cutting through service-station lots to avoid traffic at stoplights, and bounding finally over the lawn of St. Francis Hospital to take Barbara and Karen to the emer-gency entrance via a shortcut.

Karen, by then, despite the oxygen mask and mouth-to-mouth resuscitation en route to Hartford, seemed lifeless. Barbara ran with her into Emergency, to a table in what looked like a small operating room, and the emergency team took over. A nursing sister led Barbara away gently, to an adjoining room, where an admissions clerk behind a typewriter began asking the questions that had to be asked.

Before long, our "duty doctor" emerged from the room where Karen lay, and his expression telegraphed his message to Bar-bara immediately: He was going to prepare her for the worst.

He began to say that sometimes, with the best of facilities and noblest of efforts, doctors and hospitals fail—and at that point a member of the hospital's emergency room team interrupted. Karen, he reported, was breathing again.

Moments later, "the man in the red car" phoned St. Francis and asked for Emergency. He had arrived at his job and was calling to learn whether Karen had made it. "Great!" he exclaimed when given the news. Asked to identify himself, he said only, "That's all right," and hung up. He never phoned again.

Karen was still under the care of the emergency room team when I arrived. The doctors repeated to me what they had already told Barbara: Karen had suffered a typically sudden onset of a rare illness—epiglottitis, cousin of croup.

The epiglottis is the lid of the voice box—an elastic piece of cartilage behind the tongue which covers the opening of the windpipe during the act of swallowing and thus prevents food or liquid from entering the larynx, or "going down the wrong way." But Karen's epiglottis, infected by a virus, had swollen quickly, eventually closing off her windpipe altogether. She had suffocated, and her heartbeat had been arrested—for how long, no one could say.

The emergency team had gotten Karen breathing after forcing a rubber tube into her lungs, and they had administered antibiotics to counter the infection and reduce the swelling. Next step would be a tracheotomy—making an opening in her trachea, or windpipe, to enable her to breathe easily—but for the moment she was not strong enough to undergo the trauma of an operation.

I went into a telephone booth at the end of a hospital corridor, phoned Gwen Barbour, the *Press,* Barbara's parents, trying to keep my voice from breaking, and failing.

Late Monday morning, Karen was wheeled into surgery. While we paced the waiting area, our pediatrician—not the duty doctor, but our regular doctor—appeared. He spoke of epiglottitis, said he hadn't seen a case in years. "This is the thing we always worry about when a child gets croupy," he said.

We wondered then—still wonder, will always wonder—why the doctor who took our call at five-thirty that morning didn't "worry about epiglottitis" and ask us to bring Karen to the hospital right away. We also wondered why we hadn't had the wit to drive Karen to a hospital in Springfield, Massachusetts— several miles closer than Hartford—rather than phoning our pediatrician. We wondered why it hadn't occurred to us, the doctor, the police, someone, to consider an emergency trache-otomy, opening Karen's windpipe with a kitchen knife, when she stopped breathing the first time.

But even on that Monday in May we knew such wonder-ing to be futile and enervating. We knew that all the prayers and energies mustered in Karen's behalf—all the strengths and skills applied—would have to be concentrated not on yes-terday's errors, but on bringing Karen through today and to-night and tomorrow.

CHAPTER III

The Vigil

She is romping with a puppy on the grass. . . .
No, that was yesterday, I think,
    or in some other
       sunlit time
Before the cruel night
That took her breath from her,
Before the searing race
    to waiting hands
       and swift skills.

She is romping with a puppy on the grass
Somewhere in a sunlit dream, I think,
And now we wait . . .
    and watch . . .
       and wait.

When she wakes, God,
Let it be with us
And not with you.
O God
    not yet
       with you.

> Mary Jo Descy
> *Enfield, Connecticut*
> *May 1967*

Most of our memories of the next ten days in Karen's life and ours are blurred together into a single misty image of uncertainty, anguish, and hope.

The tracheotomy was a success. Barbara's mother—a nurse,

bless her—arrived at Bradley Field on a Tuesday morning flight. And as Karen was installed in a special world known as "the fog room," Barbara and I began our vigil at her bedside.

We knew only that Karen had suffered a terrible shock, that she seemed in a kind of coma and was unable to respond to us, and that her life was being sustained by science—an intravenous needle taped alternately at her wrist and ankle, nourishing her with a solution of "Dextrose 5 per cent with Electrolyte No. 75"; antibiotics fighting bacterial infection; a trach tube carrying air to her lungs; and a machine that filled her room, and her lungs, with clouds of cool, slowly swirling "fog."

There were several beds in the fog room on Dillon 3—as our pediatrics ward was known—but Karen had the room to herself. The fog room is primarily for croup cases, and the croup season, we were told, was behind us.

Karen lay alone in the fog room—or so it seemed in her first hours there. Helpless, still, uncomplaining, apparently unconcerned. Even as we held her hand, wiped her brow, whispered or sang to her, she seemed alone within herself, unaware, incapable of any emotion. Her eyes looked through us. Our voices failed to reach her. Her tiny chest rose and fell almost imperceptibly as she sucked the fog into her lungs through the metal tube protruding from her windpipe; otherwise she appeared as totally unresponsive to the world around her as a human being can be.

Barbara and I spelled one another at Karen's bedside, holding her hand, watching for some sign of recognition in her eyes, repeating those words of hers that had always made her laugh —"ride the horsey" . . . "noku" (music) . . . "take a swing" . . . "dinner ready, Daddy!" We took catnaps in the fog room and after the first day and night took turns going home to sleep—Barbara late at night, myself at midmorning.

Private-duty nurses were with Karen around the clock to administer the intravenous feeding and to hook up the bedside suction machine when Karen developed a rattle in her breathing, indicating that mucus was building up in her lungs.

The fog room doesn't do much for a nurse's appearance—wilting her uniform and destroying her hairdo—but most of our nurses remained gentle and solicitous. The one exception —a woman who seemed curiously remote from Karen's discomforts, or unaware of them—reduced Barbara to near-hysteria.

Karen had been subjected to a new horror—"seizures," which wracked her body and could best be controlled by anticonvulsant drugs. The worst of these seizures occurred when our remote-seeming nurse was on duty.

Over a period of minutes, this convulsion grew in intensity, taking control of Karen—yet even as Karen was losing her color, this nurse declined to summon a doctor. Finally, I left the fog room, found the staff nurse on the ward, implored her to call a resident. The doctor who responded to our call —a young Filipino—had to massage Karen's heart as well as administer an anticonvulsant. Despite the private-duty nursing administrator's claim that nurses for the three-to-eleven shift were extremely hard to find, I had to insist that the woman assigned to Karen during that period be replaced, somehow.

The seizures, we knew, could only be caused by some disturbance of brain function. We asked our pediatrician, who had called in a staff neurologist for consultation, to give us the verdict: Had Karen suffered some permanent brain damage?

It was too early to tell, he said, but he would guess not. We must be patient. (How often we were to hear that.)

But what could be said of Karen's condition now? Why, with her eyes wide open, could she not see us, or even follow my hand as it passed in front of her? Was she in a coma?

We received no helpful answers and sensed that the host of medical people who came to Karen's bedside feared the worst but were reluctant to reveal their fears until they could be confirmed.

Desperate to be assured that everything possible was being

done for Karen, we asked, after the fifth day at St. Francis, that a second neurologist be called in. Our request was granted, and on Karen's first Sunday afternoon in the hospital, while I was sleeping at home, Karen was examined by a neurologist from Hartford Hospital.

As the doctor reached into his bag for the crude instruments of his trade—a flashlight, a safety pin, a rubber-tipped hammer —Barbara stood at the head of Karen's bed, her brown London Fog raincoat insulating her from the chill of the fog room. She watched intently, prayerfully, as this "brain man" sought responses from Karen to his gentle probing. When the examination was finished, our consultant—whom Barbara remembers as "a soft-spoken man in a gray suit"—sat with Barbara on a bench outside the fog room and told her what he had seen.

He was not a man to raise false hopes or to rule out miracles. He said he was sorry to tell us that our child had suffered very serious damage to her brain, and for the time being at least had lost virtually all her ability to perform voluntary and involuntary functions, even including the sucking reflex. The prognosis: Karen's very chances of survival for any length of time were not good. However, there *had* been cases of unexplained, spontaneous recovery. He himself had seen them.

Shattered, but grateful for what at least were straightforward answers, Barbara sought to make the ray of hope grow brighter. What of our talking and singing to Karen? Was it all pointless —or was there some chance of our getting through to her, of awakening something within her, of keeping a thread of contact between us, of letting her know that she was not lost and would be finding her way back to us?

Well, Barbara was told, we could try. Certainly talking to her could do no harm. It might help.

When the doctor had gone, Barbara buried her head on the first available friendly shoulder—and the shoulder happened to belong to Chuck Masters. We had been acquainted with Chuck and Sally Masters through our church, the First Presbyterian Church of Enfield. Now it happened that Sally was in St. Francis for surgery, and Chuck was calling on Karen after visiting his wife. We didn't know it then, but Sally's hands were to become as valuable to us in future months as Chuck's shoulder had been on that Sunday.

We had many close friends in Enfield and were not surprised that they rallied to us during those first despairing days. Lou and Phyllis and Gail and Mary Jo neglected their own families regularly, that they might "take John for a day" or spell us at Karen's bedside so we could go to dinner together. Tim and Maureen stood by us in the hospital and asked the Association of Marian Helpers to "intervene" in Karen's behalf. Ted and Rosemary, who had stayed overnight with us less than forty-eight hours before Karen fell ill, phoned from Colorado to say, ". . . we can't find words. . . ."

We discovered, in fact, through many small but touching acts, just how many friends we really had:

A rap at the back door from Sadie, who delivered our dry cleaning. She didn't have any for us that week, but had heard about Karen and couldn't pass by without stopping to let us know we were in her prayers.

An uncharacteristically brief note from our faraway friend Fingal—"With the hope in my heart that our prayers have been answered quickly, I wait for the good news."

A huge teddy bear delivered to Karen by a huge man who stood red-eyed at her bedside. The card accompanying the bear was signed "N. Bartolotta."

A "spiritual bouquet" of holy masses, holy communions, and rosaries from Sophie, Ann, Yvonne, and Mae—the four ladies who came to the *Press* every Thursday morning to stuff and bundle the papers as they came off the press.

A beckoning sign from a female teller at our Enfield branch of the Connecticut Bank and Trust Company. "You may not remember me, but my boys were *Press* carriers and I remember how nice you were to Duane when he had open-heart surgery. I thought this might help Karen." Then she handed me a "green scapular," an image of the Immaculate Heart of Mary on green cloth, to hang on Karen's bed. We accepted it—and the next day Karen moved her head from side to side for the first time and sipped juice from a cup.

A "Dear Karen" note in purple crayon from a faraway cousin: "I hope you will get better soon. I know you are unhappy and I am unhappy too. I hope John won't catch it too. Love, Debbie."

And a long note from Beatrice Parsons, who at seventy-five continued to contribute a "Grandma Sez" column to the *Press*:

Dear Barbara and Bill:

When trouble hits one's friends, the first reaction is, "What can I possibly do to help?" and the telephone starts to ring, the doorbell as well, so that the poor beleaguered couple, in this case Barbara and Bill Breisky, are forced to live over and over their moments of tragedy.

Long years ago, this Parsons person decided to stand by in such cases, make an early call, then keep sternly away from the telephone—which is why you haven't heard from me. I have, however, eagerly questioned Phyllis each day for the latest news of Karen and of you two as well; and of course Mary Jo tells me each time she has been to St. Francis.

The day I called at your home I had a dim idea that I might baby-sit for you—but Phyllis was there, Bill was asleep and things were under control.

You are young enough to be my children so I'd like to lecture you a bit even as I would my son and his wife under the same circumstances. I want you both to think seriously about the day when Karen comes home from the hospital. She will need intelligent and unremitting care for some time and you both must be in physical shape to give it to her. You are expending so much of yourselves right now; the physical drain plus the mental anguish is sure to take its toll and it could hit right when Karen needs you most desperately.

Karen is in good hands now. There's little you can do to add to her comfort or well-being for the moment, so this is the time to build up your own strength for that time when you really can help her. Think seriously about it, will you?

I am greatly worried about you because there is a very real danger that one or both of you can reach your limit. Don't let it happen. Every one of us here at the *Press* is pulling and praying for you and for Karen, and Grandmaw loves you all very much.

With love, Bea.

Indomitable Bea.

She was right about building up our strength. We hadn't yet begun to feel exhaustion, but there was no point in seeing how far we could stretch. For the time being, we decided, no more all-night vigils in the hospital.

Bea also was right about the anguish of answering the telephone and doorbell. But even Bea couldn't have anticipated one front-door caller, whose mission, even today, stirs feelings of bitterness.

This knock on the door came within a few days of Karen's admission to St. Francis. I was at the hospital at the time, and Barbara was preparing to drive down. The visitor said he was sorry to disturb Barbara but it was necessary that she sign a paper for him. He represented an insurance company, he said, and it seemed that one of his firm's policyholders had driven the car that failed to heed N. Bartolotta's warning siren and had been struck by the police car en route to the hospital. He said he would appreciate Barbara's signing a piece of paper stating that Karen did not suffer any injury as a result of this accident.

Barbara's eyes blurred. She wanted to be rid of this man, and she signed.

I didn't know who, if anyone, was chiefly responsible for Karen's condition, but I felt at the time that the insurance company's action was contemptible, if not illegal. Still, we've never made an effort to determine even the name of the company. For a long time, the notion of suing an insurance company, of collecting any sort of payment for Karen's tragedy, seemed abhorrent. This was a wrongheaded notion, no doubt, for Karen was the one who had been hurt, and deserved compensation, and I was the one who was deciding not to consider taking any legal action.

This was a matter that I don't believe Barbara or I ever discussed, but I knew without asking just how she would feel. I knew she would believe, as I did, that if we sought compensation for Karen's injury, perhaps we would accept her problems as permanent, and not work as hard to correct them as we ought. And, of course, at that point we didn't know what her long-range problems might be.

Night and day, the Karen in the fog room remained our Sleeping Beauty. When she was truly asleep, her eyes were closed—but that seemed the only discernible difference between her periods of sleep and wakefulness. Sometimes, when she slept at night, I would prowl the quiet corridors of the hospital's public areas in search of a coffee or ice cream machine. In my prowlings I would meet hospital staff workers I didn't recognize at all, yet who would ask, "How's the little girl?" Late one night I picked up a copy of a Catholic magazine and read a story of a family made more mature and more happy since a mongoloid child was born into it: Now all the other children work together to make a full life for their gentle, loving sibling. On a hospital elevator I overheard a story of a new admission to St. Francis whose courage was inspiring to everyone who met her: Blind, and crippled with arthritis, her love of music and children was so great that she had forced her hands to play the piano and offered her services as a music teacher to blind children. And I met an ulcer-ridden bus driver who arrived at the hospital doubled up with pain, and on the day of his departure almost kicked a bedpan out of a nurse's hands to demonstrate that he was feeling fit. This bus driver had heard of Karen and wanted me to know he had prayed hard for her.

Shortly after she was examined by the second neurologist, Karen was transferred to a private room down the hall from the fog room. Her epiglottitis was under control and the trach tube removed, so she could breathe through her nose and mouth, and cry aloud. (At first she hadn't been able to cry at all. We had even been grateful when, while she still had her trach tube, she gave her first soundless cry—soundless because the air that would have created a sound in the larynx was being diverted through the trach tube.) And there had been other encouraging signs: She could swallow again, and yawn.

Very soon after the move out of the fog room, Karen was taken off intravenous feedings and started on spoonfuls of fruit juice and of milk with Karo. Aside from the joy of seeing Karen freed at last of needles and tubes, I think we were happiest of all that we were about to be permitted to pick her up. We seemed on our way to having Karen delivered back to us, and I thought it time I began keeping a notebook on her progress.

I had used odd scraps of paper to jot down occasional thoughts and questions about Karen even while she was in the fog room, but when she moved into her own room, I decided to begin keeping a more orderly record of our observations. On the first page I noted that her eyes didn't seem to respond at all to the neurologist's flashlight, but that she went slightly wild-eyed when she was picked up; that she was suffering persistent gas pains; that she seemed to be getting slightly less rigid, more willing to allow the nurses and ourselves to exercise her legs; that the I.V. catheter was out and that she was free of tubes for the first time—and that Maddy had been able to hold Karen in her lap and to feed her a few spoonfuls of orange sherbet. I concluded: "We have no idea how long we will be here, what treatment Karen will require or how effectively her condition can be treated, what problems she will have to face."

"Maddy." Today she is Mrs. Donald Swanner, of Scott City, Missouri, mother of Donald and Kimberly Swanner, but at the time she was Miss Madelene Vieira, of New Britain, Connecticut. Maddy was Karen's seven-to-three nurse, the only nurse who stayed with us throughout Karen's hospitalization, never taking a day off—and Karen was Maddy's first private-duty patient.

Maddy plainly loved Karen, and her treatment of Karen told us that love was going to play a significant role in Karen's recovery.

If Maddy is to go on record as Karen's best-remembered nurse, then Joe Crowley must be singled out as her most extraordinary doctor. Most of the physicians who treated Karen will remain nameless here, but Dr. Joseph Crowley, although he may prefer it, shall not be granted anonymity.

It was Dr. Crowley, an ear-nose-and-throat man, who had been called in to perform Karen's tracheotomy. His last official acts were to remove her trach tube and to stop in once or twice to assure that the trach wound was healing nicely. But Joe Crowley continued to call at Karen's bedside virtually every day, unofficially. His words and actions demonstrated a faith in prayer which seemed quite as strong as his faith in medical science. Barbara shed a tear or two on one of Joe Crowley's Sunday afternoon visits, and thanked him . . . and hoped his prayers didn't imply that nothing less than a miracle could bring Karen around.

Our neurologist, meanwhile, was ordering an EEG (electroencephalogram) test to measure Karen's brain waves. He told us that Karen's small signs of progress were encouraging, but that they could level off at any time, and that there might well be residual damage. An EEG now, he said, would be a good starting point in assessing the extent of the damage. He asked us if Karen had shown any signs of recognizing us yet (she hadn't); if she had held her head up yet (she hadn't); if she had always ground her teeth so furiously (only occasionally, in her sleep).

Later that day Karen was wheeled into the EEG room. Her head was measured in centimeters with a tape, and sixteen red markings made on her crown. Electrodes were attached at these points with glue and gauze, the glue quick-dried with short blasts of air. The technicians said she should be drowsy or asleep during the test, so she was given sleeping pills.

Wired up, Karen was placed on a bed in a soundproofed room, and the wires were plugged into terminals at the head of the bed. She looked as if she were getting a permanent, resting comfortably in her green p.j.'s, as the machine was turned on and a pen began to record her brain waves and muscle movements on a paper tape that moved through the machine at a rate of some fifteen inches every ten seconds. She remained completely relaxed throughout what seemed to me an ordeal, and in an hour was back in her room, taking tiny swallows of milk and Karo.

We had imagined that this EEG test was going to answer our most urgent questions for us, pinpointing the damage and perhaps indicating the therapy Karen would require. But we were mistaken. Our neurologist would only say that damage was indicated, but that it could not be measured until Karen had been observed over a period of time, and perhaps tested again.

I violated the hospital code of conduct at that point and prevailed upon a sympathetic nurse to let me read Karen's record. At the end of the record I found the EEG report. Most of it meant little to me—"no real alpha . . . some mild shifting asymmetry between hemispheres"—but four words at the end of the report seemed to confirm our worst fears: ". . . a grossly abnormal EEG . . ."

Disturbed that we were told so little of Karen's condition, and given so little to do for her, we took a step we knew to be roughly comparable to dangling a field mouse in front of the family cat: We confronted our neurologist with a medical article from a popular magazine. The article, which concerned a youngster helped by Philadelphia's Institutes for the Achievement of Human Potential, had been given us by our across-the-street neighbor, Gwen Barbour, who, it developed, had served on a "patterning team" working with a hyperactive, brain-injured ten-year-old Enfield youngster.

Our neurologist's reaction was polite but totally dampening. He said he had been schooled in Philadelphia and had colleagues down there who said they didn't think much of The Institutes. If we had two or three thousand dollars to spend ("waste," I believe was his actual word choice), we were welcome to try—but he couldn't recommend it. The Institutes' only secret, he said, was the amount of time they spent on a patient —and those hundreds of hours could be devoted to some other program, with the same or greater success.

But what "other program"? He didn't offer one.

On June 7 Karen was taken off the critical list, and because she had slept through three nights in a row, it was decided she could get along without an eleven-to-seven nurse.

Each day as we drove to St. Francis Hospital we dared hope that a kind of breakthrough would have occurred in the hours that we had been away—that Karen would speak a word or show somehow that she recognized us. Instead we were to have a time of minor ups and downs, of progress and setbacks. But Karen was taking at least a step and a half forward for each step backward.

One morning she was able to sleep on her stomach for the first time, and our neurologist said, "She's coming along nicely."

Early one afternoon she showed her first real signs of an appetite, and Maddy got her to eat a baby food jar of peaches. The evening nurse tried a jar of "turkey dinner," and Karen took it and went to sleep—but at seven she awoke suddenly and vomited undigested food in her bed. The resident doctor who responded to the nurse's call was a young woman. She said she guessed Karen just wasn't ready for "turkey dinner," and she found a word for Karen's state of consciousness—"stupor."

One day we asked the third member of our pediatrician's group practice, as we had asked others without success, "Is Karen conscious?"

She has some degree of consciousness, he told us, or she couldn't react to food in her mouth by swallowing. And the fact that a flashlight can cause the pupils of her eyes to contract indicates that in a sense she "sees." He said it was important to keep her well nourished, and that we must guard against pneumonia by turning her, or holding her in a sitting position.

Virtually the entire staff of Dillon 3 greeted Barbara when

she arrived on the morning of June 6. "Karen is smiling!" they reported.

"Giggling" was closer to the truth. We were overjoyed.

Karen had seemed rigid and obstreperous when Maddy tried to feed her breakfast that morning, and Maddy had put her down and stepped out into the hall for a moment. When Maddy returned, Karen was wearing what Maddy termed "a funny expression."

"What's going on, honey?" Maddy inquired—and Karen broke into a giggle.

Barbara phoned home with the good news, urging me to bring my camera, and soon the news was spread to all corners of our world.

Our neurologist declared that the smiling was "a good sign." And he had more good news for us: Karen had "lost her Babinski," a Babinski reflex being a toe-flexing action evoked by stroking the sole of the foot. Infants normally lose this immature neurological action before their first birthday—but two-year-old Karen's had returned on May 22.

Well, I wrote in my notebook, you lose a Babinski, you gain a giggle. A happy balance indeed.

But the giggling was a one-day phase which remains unexplained to this day. Had Karen merely suffered a pinched funny bone? We don't know. In any case we weren't to see even a suggestion of a smile again for a couple of weeks.

The clergyman who had baptized Karen at First Presbyterian drove the eighteen miles to St. Francis almost daily, to say a prayer for her. We told him we were grateful, but that he mustn't feel obliged to come so often. He smiled. "Children are pretty important," he said—and he continued to make the daily trip.

Frequently we had to settle for half-shift nurses on the three-to-eleven shift: The hospital could only find part-timers—house-wife-RN's, usually—and at times we were without a nurse from three to seven or seven to eleven. Often during those hours our friend Sheila Kealey would appear on the scene to relieve

Barbara or myself, announcing, "Sheila, mother of Jimmy, reporting for duty."

One three-to-eleven shift I was alone with Karen. After Karen had eaten some supper, a nurse's aide I recall only as "Miss Anderson"—the inscription on her name tag—came into the room and asked if she might look after Karen so that I could go to the cafeteria for a meal.

Miss Anderson had gone out of her way to be helpful to us whenever she was on duty, so when I returned from supper I told her how much we had appreciated her help. She pointed to a neck scar I hadn't noticed until then—the faint reminder of a tracheotomy incision—and said, "I remember what my father went through when I had this operation."

During Karen's third and final week at St. Francis, there were few perceptible changes in her condition.

For a couple of days she cried every time we sat her up, so we had to find a way of feeding her in a supine position. An eyedropper proved the best means of getting milk into her mouth.

Another day she suffered a succession of "stomach cramps" —cause unexplained—and couldn't keep any food down.

On June 8 Karen was handed Nicky Bartolotta's teddy bear, and she seemed to grasp it—twice.

Two days later we thought she was beginning to show some response to our voices, to comforting words. We also noted that she had begun exploring the outside world with her tongue.

On June 12 and 13 Karen was wheeled to Physical Therapy and given an evaluation. She protested loudly at a series of what seemed to be joint-loosening exercises, but at session's end appeared as relaxed as she had ever been in the hospital. We were given some passive exercises to do with her—and then we were told that we could take Karen home the next day.

Home! We yearned to have Karen home and to be a family again. We had no doubts about our ability to satisfy her basic needs, but on the other hand, we had no precise course charted for her or for ourselves, and we had been given very little to do for her. The fog room on Dillon 3, for all its health-restoring qualities, had been chill and gray and somehow bewildering, forbidding. Karen's world at home, in the late spring in New England, would be warm and scented with the apple blossoms outside her window. Yet something of the fog room was still with us. Karen remained enveloped in a kind of fog, and we had not yet been assured that we would succeed in cutting through this barrier.

CHAPTER IV

"Hi"

The two-year-old daughter we brought home from St. Francis Hospital was in many ways like a new baby. But she was a bundle of joy who had had the joy knocked out of her, and she was going to require considerably more attention than a new and healthy baby if she was to overcome her setback. Even her new Easter bunny was much the worse for wear, having developed a permanent sag after more than a week in the fog room.

The Dillon 3 staff gathered to say good-by to our Sleeping Beauty, and the head nurse declared, "We hate to see her go." We didn't share that attitude, but we appreciated the thought.

Karen seemed surprisingly relaxed on the trip home, in Barbara's lap. There was no siren this time. We drove slowly, over back roads, speaking little but thinking our private thoughts of previous trips home with new additions to the family. It had been four years since we brought baby John home to a rented bungalow in the Thompsonville section of Enfield. Barbara, as bookkeeper, circulation manager and advertising salesman of the down-at-the-heels little newspaper operation we had mortgaged our souls for, ten months previous, had toiled twelve hours a day until she was two weeks overdue with our No. 1 child, and John, a ten-pound baby, seemed to have thrived on that regimen. In John's first four years we had started a second publication; our newspaper staff had grown to twenty and our family to five. And half a year before Karen fell ill we had begun the process of transferring ownership of the *Press* into the hands of an upstate New York newspaperman. We had bought our 1813 house on lower Enfield Street, and I had agreed to maintain a desk at the *Press* as a sort of columnist-consultant-handy-man for a year, with plenty of time off to woo the muses from my ivory tower at home, in behalf of assorted free-lance writing projects.

It was a blessing that I would be able to work at home, I thought, as I carried Karen—at twenty-three pounds a full seven pounds lighter than when we took her to the hospital—up the steps of our vine-shaded back porch, through the rear of the house to the sofa bed which had been made up for her in the living room.

As the day of her homecoming wore on, we convinced ourselves that Karen was responding to the sounds and smells—if not the sights—of home. At any rate, she had a very comfortable day. She ate well. Some close friends stopped by. And John, who had driven with us to St. Francis a few times but had not been permitted to visit his sister's room, saw her for the first time in more than three weeks.

"She's looking at me," John said simply, "but she doesn't talk."

We couldn't bring ourselves to tell him, just then, that while Karen's eyes were wide open, she wasn't really "looking" at him at all.

John had for some time been promised a set of bunk beds so that he, as our lone boy child, might on special occasions invite a friend to sleep over. We bought the set just before Karen was released from St. Francis, and John agreed immediately when we asked if we might borrow one for Karen "until she gets better."

The borrowed bunk bed was installed in the playroom, a tiny room directly behind the kitchen and directly beneath my office. The bunk railing was put on this bed, and the room became Karen's daytime headquarters—and the focal point of our lives.

John was in nursery school at the time, and on Karen's first full day at home he invited Danny, his best friend from school, to come and meet his sister. John didn't realize what a favor he was doing us: Danny brought his mother, who was to become one of Karen's most enthusiastic "patterning ladies."

Karen's grandmother, otherwise known as Nana, had had to return to Philadelphia before Karen was released from the hospital, and now Nana Liz, a much beloved relative by marriage, was with us, to see that Gretchen and John were not neglected.

John related with fascination how his "plain Nana" (as he called her, to distinguish her from "Nana Liz") had cooked some flowers (nasturtiums) for his dinner while Karen was in the hospital. Nana Liz replied that the best she could manage was her special plum cake. Life was returning to normal—or at least our new version of normal, which meant that we could begin to concern ourselves once again with everyday joys and problems, while shaping our reordered way of life.

Karen had someone with her throughout her waking hours, talking and singing to her, feeding her, administering the simple "passive exercises" we had been taught at St. Francis, searching for signs of small victories. The weeks ahead were to be weeks of watching, listening, measuring, persevering.

In the hospital Karen had seemed truly comfortable only when lying on her side. At home she continued to prefer this posture, but with a slight difference: instead of lying motionless, she commenced waving her free arm in the air from time to time.

On her third day at home, a smile. Not an activated funny bone this time, but an honest-to-goodness responsive expression of joy. John and I had been doing a comedy routine which before Karen's illness had always meant surefire merriment. The first few tries brought little or no response. But then Doc chimed in with a howl or two—and Karen smiled. Two days later, we were able to induce a smile with a tickle.

We could feel a growing alertness in Karen. We knew she couldn't see us, yet whenever someone with a familiar voice would enter the room and speak to her, she seemed to make an effort to "look" in the direction of that voice.

Sight, however, was not the only one of Karen's senses that

was totally disorganized because her brain's oxygen supply had been cut off: she had also become, temporarily at least, hyposensitive. This meant her sense of touch had been impaired, her pain threshold raised to the point where she had very little early-warning signal to advise us that she had been bruised, jabbed, stung, or bent out of shape. We had to be all the more careful to assure that she didn't injure herself.

This impairment didn't mean she was unable to cry, however. Although she had no apparent recurrence of seizures, she cried more often than she smiled—sometimes almost hysterically—but was unable to tell us why. The worst of her crying spells occurred around mealtime and continued for some twenty minutes. Our pediatrician attributed these spells to stomach cramps, and we tried to control them with a liquid tranquilizer.

The tranquilizer helped, but the solution, Barbara swears, proved to be food—"real food," as opposed to baby food. First we tried a box of animal crackers. I held one in her mouth, and nibble by nibble she consumed it—and three more. A few days later, after Nana Liz had gone home and fifteen-year-old Käthe Kirchmeier had signed on as mother's helper for the summer, Karen screamed and struggled through another of her prescribed "junior baby food" meals. Both Barbara and Käthe were exhausted by the ordeal and retired to the living room with the cheeseburgers Barbara had prepared for them. Karen, in Barbara's lap, seemed interested in her mother's lunch, and when Barbara held the cheeseburger in front of her mouth and offered it to her, Karen virtually lunged for it.

Barbara gasped as Karen took a sizable bite, chewing and swallowing slowly but obviously with enormous satisfaction. Had the cheeseburger aroma attracted her? Was her sense of smell working overtime to compensate for the loss of other senses? Did she have stored-up memories of favorite foods? Had she recalled what a cheeseburger was when Barbara, not really expecting any reaction, had asked if she would like a taste?

These questions were racing through Barbara's mind as she

declared to Käthe, "Why, she was just hungry. *That's* why she's been crying."

Dr. Joe Crowley, on his way home from a visit to the nearby Connecticut State Prison, paid us a surprise visit that day and was obliged to listen to every detail of the Great Cheeseburger Event. He seemed impressed by Karen's slight improvements, unimpressed by Barbara's faith in cheeseburger therapy, and sorry to have to say good-by. He told us he was going to the University of Minnesota for a year's study in inner-ear surgery and would try to keep in touch.

We had written to The Institutes in Philadelphia shortly after we brought Karen home from the hospital, and on June 27 I received a reply stating their waiting list was so regrettably long that they could not see Karen until May of 1969, or twenty-three months hence. We were dismayed but not depressed by this news, assuring ourselves either that we could arrange an earlier appointment somehow or that Karen might not require any long-range help after all.

But we devoured some literature Barbara's mother obtained from The Institutes, searching for ideas we could put into practice. In one article reprint, The Institutes' Carl Delacato wrote that brain-damaged children could be helped by keeping them on their stomachs, on the floor, and urged to crawl. We put Karen on the playroom floor immediately, and that same day she developed a knack, somehow, for inching herself backward, her legs kicking feebly and futilely.

That same week, eight-month-old Gretchen learned to sit up, putting her a notch ahead of her twenty-six-month-old sister. And Karen paid her first post-hospital visit to our pediatrician.

The doctor was "especially encouraged" by Karen's use of her legs, but said he would like to see her able to hold up her head. He borrowed our literature about The Institutes and declared (despite the neurologist's negative reaction), "We can learn about their work together." Karen's weight that day was twenty-eight pounds—still two pounds less than when she became ill—

but the doctor considered this weight loss "good, considering what she's been through."

"What Karen had been through" began haunting Barbara that summer in the form of a vivid, recurring nightmare. Her nostrils would be assaulted once again, in a dream wherein the police car heater churned up dry, dusty air—and she could see Karen stiffening and turning blue, the sudden crush of traffic on Interstate 91, the screech of brakes and a cut on Nicky Bartolotta's forehead, popcorn on the floor of the red car as it raced toward St. Francis. . . .

Work proved the best antidote for nightmares. We were grateful that literature concerning The Institutes suggested things we could do for Karen. Stimulation seemed a key, so we began a stimulative program, rubbing her arms and legs first with ice cubes, then with a warm towel. We pinched and tickled her. We scrubbed her arms and hands with a vegetable brush. And, of course, we kept her on the floor.

Early the next month (July) Karen managed a series of baby steps forward. She discovered a thumb and put it in her mouth. She decided she liked being on the floor and learned to push herself up onto her elbows. Her screaming spells decreased in frequency if not in duration, and a nurse friend told us, "I wouldn't be surprised if some of it isn't just plain frustration. She must feel a little bit lost. She just doesn't know what to do with herself."

One morning we found Karen, alone, making contented "mmmmm" sounds to herself. They seemed her first expression of happiness other than the occasional smile or giggle. The next day Barbara and Karen, resting on the back-porch chaise, had a long "conversation," even though Karen didn't say a word. Karen was *trying* to talk, Barbara insisted.

Certainly the number of sounds she could make was increasing, and there was no mistaking the fact that she was becoming more responsive to her family. By early July she would virtually leap for joy whenever I entered the playroom and called her name. Her head would rise from the bed, and her legs would kick in the air, all to the accompaniment of a happy squeal.

Karen told us, without uttering a word, that she needed to be held, touched, stroked, patted. Her rigidity diminished slowly, and as it did we became more confident about handling her.

If Barbara's first intuitive contribution to Karen's well-being was cheeseburger therapy, mine was "whee" therapy.

All fathers toss their children into the air and shout "whee," I suppose. It's instinctive behavior, or at least role behavior that is tolerated by most societies. Yet friends and relatives—virtually everyone but Barbara—winced when I commenced swinging Karen, then tossing her gently into the air, soon after she was released from the hospital. I don't really recall my motivation; I believe I was primarily hopeful of re-establishing old patterns and of "loosening Karen up." Visitors to the house seemed terrified that I would drop her—but I persisted, and events bore out the soundness of my instinct, if not my reasoning.

Karen was happy on the playroom floor, but she was even happier lying on her tummy on a blanket beneath one of our backyard apple trees. She loved the soft, summery breezes—but she didn't, when she first encountered it, have any enthusiasm for grass.

The form of vegetation known as grass seems green and soft and restful if you're admiring it from a rocking chair on your front porch or running across it in a new pair of sneakers. But when, without warning, you are placed on a rather bristly lawn for the first time after your eyes have lost their ability to see, and your stored-up memories of grass have been pretty well obliterated, you might well be terrified by grass. At least that's what seemed to happen to Karen.

We thought, in fact, that we heard her say "ow."

We also thought during the next day or two—and desperately wanted to believe—that we heard her make sounds approximating "ma-ma," "da-da," and "hi."

Barbara had worked especially hard on "hi."

"Hi, Karen. . . . Hi. . . . Can you say 'hi,' too? . . . Hi, Karen. . . ."

Karen managed to produce an audible *h* sound, but couldn't connect it to the *i* at first. Certainly she was trying to talk, but her tongue appeared to get in the way. Sometimes she would squeeze her lips together, then part them slightly, as if trying to shape a word, and would succeed only in producing some very wet bubbles and a faint sound, as if to say, "Phooey—talking is too much trouble."

But then, finally, softly, without advance fanfare, the "hi" did come. Barbara and Karen had been sitting on our green love seat, carrying on the ritual one-sided conversation for as long as Karen would pay attention. She *wanted* to speak, Barbara sensed that day, because she seemed to be concentrating so hard on Barbara's endless repetition of "hi" phrases.

"Hi," said Karen.

One lone word had been uttered, but what Karen had communicated was "Hi, Mommy. . . . Hello, world. . . . Remember me?" And a mutual recognition of the moment's meaning was expressed eloquently in the mother-daughter hugs and smiles that followed.

One Friday in mid-July, after a particularly "aware" evening, when she had made a sound that closely resembled "na-na," Karen had a bad night. She was awake and fussing for most of the night, yet she didn't seem sick in any way. Barbara had a hunch that, excited by her achievements, Karen simply was too keyed-up to sleep.

The following day, July 18, Karen delivered not a single word, but a whole sentence: "Hi . . . Da-da." She said it loud and clear and often. There could be no doubting it now—Karen would speak again.

There also was no doubting her acute sense of hearing. She would suddenly become fearful, apprehensive, or simply intent, and we would wonder why. Then we would become aware that a dog was barking, a power mower had been started, a far-off siren was wailing. We, too, had heard these sounds, but they hadn't registered on our consciousness until Karen called our attention to them.

I had been told by our neurologist, as he examined Karen's eyes in the hospital, that vision was likely to be one of the least of her problems—the function least likely to suffer permanent impairment. But he said he couldn't begin to guess whether or when she would be able to speak again, or walk, or use her hands. So we were overjoyed by "Hi, Da-da," and spurred on to help bring back her other functions.

On the day of "Hi, Da-da," we began putting Karen through a rather crude version of what The Institutes refer to as "homo-lateral patterning." With some guidance from our friend and neighbor Gwen Barbour, who had served on a patterning team, and a few clues from the literature we had received from The Institutes, we began a patterning exercise that approximated the first crawling motion a baby normally makes—the right arm and leg moving forward in unison, then the left arm and leg, while the head moves from side to side.

Patterning Karen demanded three sets of arms—"one to do the right side," we explained to volunteers, "one to do the left, and one to do the head." Karen, as we understood it, was not required to co-operate. She was being programmed. Since her brain was damaged in such a way that it was unable to send out sophisticated signals telling her to move her arms and legs, we would send those signals back to the brain by manipulating her limbs in a simulation of crawling. Hopefully, the healthy cells of her brain would register this activity and establish new path-ways for the signals that direct these movements, so that even-tually Karen would be able to crawl all by herself.

Our patterning was done on a dinette table. Barbara, Käthe, myself, and a number of our friends took turns "doing the sides." Nana Liz specialized in doing the head, having per-fected a technique for stroking Karen's cheek and brushing the hair away from her face with each turn of the head.

Four initial patterning problems were rhythm (finding three people who could work in near-perfect unison), Karen's bel-

lowing, our backaches, and John. We gradually solved the
rhythm and bellowing problems by patterning Karen to music,
and the backache problem by raising the table a few inches.
The problem with John was that he was certain we were tor-
turing his sister, and we could only convince him otherwise by
putting him up on the table and patterning him.

At first Karen seemed inclined to agree that patterning was a
form of torture. She screamed. I said perhaps we had better
stop; we might be hurting her. Barbara insisted, through gritted
teeth, that we continue.

What Karen liked best about patterning, after she had re-
signed herself to it, was the bell on our timer, telling us we had
reached the end of a session. "Bell!" she learned to shout, and
we were meant to call a halt, then and there.

Karen didn't demonstrate immediately the effectiveness of
patterning. The first time she did move herself, in fact, it was in
an irregular circle, rather than directly forward or backward.
She would awaken us at night with a cry, and we would go to
her bed to find her wedged into a corner and unable to work
her way out.

Her vocabulary, however, grew rapidly, and her diction improved with it. "Hi, Da-da" became "Hi, Daddy." Then came
"night-night," "by-by," "milk," and, of course, "no."

One lunchtime, Barbara announced that Karen had added
"wet" to her vocabulary. When I tried to coax Karen into
demonstrating her new word, she pursed her lips, then suddenly swung her legs, kicking a cup of coffee out of my hands
and onto the sofa and rug. I got my "wet."

Then came her first pairs of words—"don't cry" and "no
cookie." Occasionally these were shortened to "don't" and
"noke," but we didn't quibble.

Late one afternoon as July drew to a close, Karen was repeating "daddy" over and over when her brother John appeared on
the scene.

"Why don't you learn to say 'Johnny'?" he asked—almost
demanded.

"Johnny" was the next word Karen uttered. John was overjoyed.

As she added other words to her vocabulary, she demonstrated that she could use them intelligently, rather than simply repeating after us. If we held to her lips a training cup filled with milk, she might say "milk," "cold," or "more," depending on the circumstances.

A wise and boundlessly energetic friend of ours, Dolly Bean, had a definition for Karen's mental prowess at that time—"submerged intelligence." Dolly was right, and she was determined to help us bring Karen's intelligence to the surface.

Dolly was an earwitness to Karen's submerged intelligence one day when she phoned our house and Barbara, deciding it was time to get Karen reacquainted with the telephone, held the receiver to Karen's ear while Dolly spoke. Karen listened intently and finally declared, with no prompting, "Nana."

Her association of the Nana-like voice on the phone with the voice of a Nana she had not spoken to since before her illness seemed of great significance, and began to bring home to us a fact none of our doctors had taken the pains to point out— that brain injury need not mean a loss of intelligence. Karen began giving us clues to her alertness soon after we got her home, and Dolly Bean and others helped us interpret those clues.

We were inexpressibly relieved and grateful for such clues, having spent agonizing hours at St. Francis wondering if Karen might remain mentally childlike because her brain cells had briefly been denied the oxygen they demand.

Our definition of "retardation" also began to be reshaped that summer by the surprising number of people in our community who, expressing their sympathy, revealed (or "confessed") that someone close to them had suffered a similar tragedy. Although I had admired and aided the Enfield Society for Retarded Children—giving their activities considerable space in the *Press* and designating them when I won an award and was asked to name my "favorite charity"—I really had little appreciation of how many families in our town, our neighborhood, our church, our own circle of friends, had been touched by that vastly misunderstood and whispered word, "retardation."

We began to appreciate that retardation could mean many things, any number of things. At any rate, we found the word repellent and we certainly weren't prepared to apply it to Karen.

Interestingly, the two sets of parents in town who seemed to talk most freely about brain injury were those who had been to The Institutes and had been given a program of activities to help them cope with and overcome their problems.

Enfield's assistant superintendent of schools, visiting Karen in the hospital, told us of a supermarket owner in our town whose teen-aged daughter had some balance and mobility problems. She could walk. She could read. Yet she couldn't run, or ride a bike, and these people in Philadelphia thought perhaps her mobility would improve if, through patterning, she learned to crawl and creep properly.

Did this youngster's problem really relate to ours? We were trying to pattern Karen because she had lost all her ability to perform voluntary functions—could scarcely move, much less crawl. This other child was being put through a crawling drill because she had a running and bike-riding problem. Her situation seemed terribly remote from Karen's, so we didn't even phone her parents to exchange ideas—until years later.

We did, however, at Gwen Barbour's urging, make contact with the parents of Timmy, the ten-year-old Enfield boy Gwen had helped pattern. Timmy's mother assembled one of her patterning teams for us and asked her son to put his bike down and go through his paces for the Breiskys. (Because of Timmy's size, his patterning teams consisted of five people—one for each arm and each leg and one for the head—and rhythm was that much more difficult.) Timmy submitted willingly to the demonstration, and afterward led us to the basement to have a look at his "crawl box"—a heavy wooden frame, open at two ends and crisscrossed with rope on the top. The frame forced him, we were told, to keep his head and stomach down when he crawled under it.

A week later, inspired by our visit with Timmy's family, we drove to Philadelphia for a visit with Nana and Grandpop and tried to "crash" The Institutes.

Barbara felt we should wait our turn; I was impatient. Our strategy, I decided, would be to place a call to the IAHP, tell them we had been patterning Karen for several weeks, had read all their literature we could lay our hands on, had visited another family that was on their program, and would be grateful for a few pointers, at least, until such time as they could give Karen a complete evaluation.

"We're here in Philadelphia," I said over the phone to a staff member at The Institutes. "Could you just have a look at Karen?"

They were sorry—but no. They simply had no time. And when a child's brain has been hurt severely, I was told, there's no such thing as a quick evaluation.

I was disappointed, even disillusioned. I found it difficult to accept the fact that no one on the staff—no one—could find half an hour for Karen.

"Do we really want to wait until the middle of next year," I asked Barbara, "to find out whether this is the best place for Karen? Suppose we decide it isn't?" Neither of us could answer that question, or had any sensible alternative to waiting.

Though we didn't get into The Institutes, we did get to see Pat Kofka. Barbara's mother had learned that Pat, a high school classmate of Barbara's, had worked at The Institutes after earning her RN and before retiring to be a mother.

Pat, Barbara, Nana, Karen and I spent an afternoon on the old Karastan carpet in Nana and Grandpop's living room, trying to adapt to Karen's situation what Pat had learned and practiced during her brief career at The Institutes.

What Barbara particularly appreciated about Pat Kofka was her enthusiasm. Pat and Barbara had been cheerleaders together at Philadelphia's Lincoln High, and Barbara was grate-

ful to find that Pat was as bubbly as ever, approaching Karen
with the same effervescence that she had displayed at basketball
games. Pat had seen a great many hurt kids at The Institutes,
and as a result of that experience she saw in Karen a potential
and a challenge rather than an object of pity. Karen's responsive-
ness—her "hi's" and giggles and willingness to co-operate—impressed Pat, and Pat's enthusiasm, in turn, heartened all of us.

"Karen is great," Pat said. "There are a lot of things she can
do, a lot of things you can do with her."

Constrict the pupils of Karen's eyes with a flashlight, Pat said
—quickly, one eye at a time, four times a day. Build a wooden
slide, she urged us, and keep Karen on it much of the time, encouraging her to crawl downhill by pinching one leg while letting her push against your hand with the other foot. Pat
showed us how to use a plastic "space mask" which covered
Karen's nose and mouth. By rebreathing, for sixty-second periods,
the carbon dioxide she exhaled, Karen could, Pat said, get a
richer supply of oxygen to her brain. (Barbara was nervous
about "masking" and tried it only rarely.)

Pat also told us of a long-shot opportunity to get Karen into
The Institutes ahead of her turn. For children from the Philadelphia area, there was a "cancellation list." Pat felt, despite
our Connecticut address, that if both of us were prepared to
spend a full week in Philadelphia, given only twenty-four hours'
notice, we might get on this list, to be called when another
family was forced to cancel. There was no guarantee Karen
would get called, but the fact that she was only two might work
in her favor. The Institutes liked to see children when they
were infants, when their hurt brains still had some developing
to do.

We got on the cancellation list. We returned to Enfield and I
built a slide which dominated one corner of our dining room.
Meanwhile, Barbara searched for books that would tell us more
about brain-injured children. One was the story of another
Karen, a profound story of courage and faith in a not-so-long-
ago time when brain-injured kids were meant to be hidden

away in dark corners—but it also was a story of a little girl who grew up relying on crutches and braces and a football helmet when she walked. Another book told the story of a cerebral-palsied child—a physician's daughter—who had gone to The Institutes and had learned to walk without any dependence on prosthetic devices.

All roads seemed to be pointing toward The Institutes for us, as we heard from friends of friends—one in Kansas, one in Ontario—who had "been helped by patterning." Yet despite this mounting evidence, I began making inquiries about other clinics or facilities where children with injured brains could be helped. There could be no harm in hedging our bets, I felt. And suppose our neurologist was right about The Institutes? After all, we had since been advised by a friend who had once handled public relations for a state association for mental retardation that The Institutes directors were said to be charlatans, given to making extravagant claims and promises.

Our social life during that season of rebuilding was a Karen-oriented social life—friends stopping over for tea or a beer to talk with Karen or about Karen. Talking had never seemed so important to us. If Karen remained unable to see us or to walk to us, at least she could communicate with us—and that was a very big "at least."

Many of the words Karen rediscovered first were, not surprisingly, words denoting objects or activities that gave her pleasure. "Ring bell." "Peek!"

Bath time, a favorite game before she fell ill, had been an ordeal when we brought Karen home from St. Francis. But by the end of the summer, she was enjoying bath time almost as much as ever, even though she had to lie supine in the tub, her head propped up on John's plastic turtle. The minute one of us would start up the stairs with her in the evening after dinner, she would squeal, "Bath! Bath! Bath!" And then "Soap! Cup! Brush!"

Her first three-word sentence made no sense to us then, nor

does it now. "Hi, man," she said one morning. "Don't fall, man!" The new sentence, enunciated clearly, was repeated throughout the day: "Hi, man. Don't fall, man! Hi, man. . . ." She declined to disclose who "man" was, or where he fell, but for several hours she seemed to find his predicament a subject of boundless fascination.

Karen relished the words for objects she began "finding" with her right hand. "Nose." "Chair." "Cup." "Tummy."

And "paper." A crinkly piece of waxed paper was a favorite toy.

"Noku" was another new word. (Why, if Karen's memory had been pretty much wiped out, was she saying "noku" again, rather than "music"?)

And "meo"—for Larry and Flo D'Aleo's piano which Karen joyously discovered with her right hand one evening.

And "post office." The two-block hike to our neighborhood post office, with Karen propped up on pillows in John's stake wagon, was a highlight of the day for her—and for her father.

And "horsey." The hobbyhorse rides she once enjoyed had become an uncertain business. Now we had to put her feet in the stirrups, help wrap her fingers around the handles, and hold her in place. But she loved these "horsey rides" and improved slowly in her ability to hold on, despite the fact that even holding her head upright was a problem. Karen had very little head control at the time, and largely for this reason could not even sit in her high chair for long without toppling sideways. (We tied lengths of toweling around her to hold her in position.)

"Can't do it!" became a favorite expression. When asked to have a go at something new or difficult, Karen would scowl and declare, "Can't do it." But she would be disappointed if we didn't insist that she try again, and there were times when she had so much confidence that she would say, at patterning time, "I take the head!"

Sometimes she really couldn't do what we asked of her; other times she could, but needed to be convinced she could. Every slight achievement was marked with applause and a round of kisses, and Karen's first thought at such a time was invariably "Show Daddy!" or "Show Mommy!"—depending on who had been with her when the accomplishment was recorded.

The more her language skills improved, the more she craved being shown that she was loved—by Mommy, Daddy, even Doc of the cold, wet nose. Her emotions were maturing rapidly, and all of a sudden her feelings could be bruised, resulting inevitably in a protruding lower lip. She was a two-year-old again.

When Daddy's late-October birthday rolled around that year, Barbara and John sang, "Happy Birthday, dear Dad-dy."

Then Karen joined in the celebration. "Happy Daddy!" she said.

She was right.

We gave Karen a flute-shaped whistle for my birthday. She was able to hold it to her mouth, but after several days' coaxing and coaching remained unable to make a noise with it. "Can't do it," she insisted. But one day, left alone, she did toot it, and thereupon went on a week-long toot.

Toward the end of November, we received a phone call that gave all of us something to toot about.

"This is The Institutes calling. . . . We have a cancellation. . . . Can you have Karen in Philadelphia at eight-thirty on the morning of November twenty-seventh?"

CHAPTER V

The Institutes

Our five-day evaluation session in the weathered, tree-shaded buildings at 8801 Stenton Avenue, in the Chestnut Hill section of Philadelphia, was in many respects the most mind-roiling, most relentlessly stimulating, most challenging week of our lives. It was also rather tiring.

Karen loved it.

The Institutes for the Achievement of Human Potential is housed in a neighborhood of sprawling, fenced-in estates created by the rich and very rich in an era before the Sixteenth Amendment declared personal income to be taxable. Today, ironically, non-profit, tax-free institutions occupy the largest of these estates.

Most of the buildings that comprise the IAHP—or simply "The Institutes"—are set among birch and dogwood, tall oaks and pines, perched above a deep ravine. For the past two decades, this grouping of small individual "institutes"—some concerned with severely hurt kids such as Karen, others with brain-related reading and learning disabilities, and with research and clinical investigation—have occupied the old stone buildings that once merely housed a family and its staff of servants. But for our initial days at The Institutes, the half-dozen imposing buildings on the former Clark estate were for the most part silent, as virtually the entire Institutes staff gathered in a compact and relatively new one-story building known as the Evaluation Center. For five long days they would concentrate all their knowledge and energies on a roomful of children whose brains had been assaulted in cruel and countless ways, and whose parents had come to see if these controversial, daringly unorthodox therapists could find a means of putting healthy but dormant brain cells to good use—find, in effect, keys to unlock the shackles that kept their children immobile, the tiny but impenetrable screens that blocked the sunlight, the vaults where the secrets of speech were stored.

Every second week, we learned, The Institutes staff goes through one of these exhausting evaluation periods, working from early morning until late at night with youngsters who, we concluded, had just two things in common: their brains had been hurt, and no doctors or therapists had been able to overcome the hurt.

For The Institutes staff, it was a week of probing, measuring, lecturing, and programming. For us (and I'm presuming to speak for most of the parents who have been through evaluation week on Stenton Avenue), it was a week of listening, questioning, absorbing, and hoping.

I don't remember how the weather was on that first day at The Institutes, or what we wore, or what ran through our minds as we drove there in our '65 Dodge from Barbara's parents' home, or even how Karen behaved or reacted. But I do remember, above all else, the sense of relief we felt as soon as we arrived there. These people at The Institutes *understood*. They knew, almost intuitively, what we had been through. They didn't waste time on sympathy; instead they offered their minds, and their eyes, ears, and hands, to formulate a massive battle plan that Barbara and myself and our friends might carry out. All of the problems that Karen had, or would face in her future, they had seen before, in other combinations.

They were happy to see Karen. They knew how to carry her, how to talk to her, how to make her comfortable, and how to make her exert herself.

They knew we asked only one thing of them—to help us make Karen well—so they made us a promise, a guarantee. They promised to exert every resource at their disposal in Karen's behalf. They guaranteed us that if they failed it would not be for lack of trying, and that meant trying until long after the five o'clock whistle had blown. And they said they would have to insist that we try just as hard, or harder.

We began our first day at The Institutes in the Evaluation Center's crowded but efficient waiting room. There were upholstered benches along three of the walls, and overhead shelves with one compartment per family—space enough for scarves, mittens and hats, diaper bags and notebooks. There was a small kitchen area, with complimentary sandwiches and beverages available at all hours. And there was a warm, carpeted floor, where the children—those who were able—were encouraged to crawl and play.

In our group of fourteen children, several appeared helpless, and two seemed so bright and well co-ordinated that their problems were in no way perceptible to us. We sized one another up, wondering about the histories of the other children, how they had got the way they were. But the curiosity within most of us, the desire to communicate our fears and hopes, seemed blocked that morning by our reticence, inhibitions, or manners. We remained polite strangers sharing a common problem and challenge.

Not many cheerful faces were to be found in that room that morning. It seemed apparent that most of these families had been through years of almost unrelieved discouragement.

There was Victor, who lay helpless in his father's lap and was fed through a plastic tube. There was a little boy from West Germany whose father, a Luftwaffe captain, crawled around the floor urging his young son forward. There was a farmer from Missouri and an osteopath from central Pennsylvania. And there was a husky teen-aged boy from Long Island who watched hungrily as I took a bite from a ham sandwich and who, when he could control the urge no longer, lunged across the room and attempted to snatch the sandwich from my hands.

Soon a staff member with a clipboard appeared in a doorway and said, "Karen Breisky?"—and our evaluation began.

First Karen's history was taken, and the questions went back to before her birth.

"Did you take any medication during pregnancy, Mrs. Breisky, when you were carrying Karen?"

"Just vitamins."

"What kind of anesthesia were you given?"

"Ether."

"Was Karen's birth cry immediate?"

"I suppose so. I wasn't told."

Then came other questions, in other rooms, to help determine Karen's ability to see, hear, move, talk, comprehend.

"How old are you, Karen?" asked Sandra Brown, an inventive RN with a knack for reaching each child almost instantly with a concerned, almost conspiratorial manner.

"I want the kitchen," declared Karen. She understood the question, but she was determined to revisit the source of drinks and sandwiches.

"Do you want to stay here with me or see the other kids?"

A smile. "See the kitchen again!"

Karen had not "seen" the kitchen at all, of course. To "see" a thing meant to Karen to visit it, smell it, touch it. Even before Philadelphia, Karen had taught us there was more than one way to see an object; The Institutes would show us she could learn more than we suspected by tactile means, relying solely on the nerve endings in her fingers to recognize objects.

Elaine Lee measured Karen's tactile competence by introducing her to a series of small objects—a stone, a ball, a whistle, a block and a soldier—closing Karen's fingers on each and describing its shape and weight.

"Now, Karen, can you pick up the ball and throw it?"

Karen groped, gripped the block, then released it. "Throw the ball!" she said.

"No, dear—that was the block. Can you try again?"

A pause, then a cheer. "I got the ball!"

"Good, Karen. . . . Now, can you feel the whistle? . . ."

We asked various members of The Institutes staff about their backgrounds and found doctors, nurses, physical therapists, a psychologist, a sociologist. But except for the doctors, they didn't use these titles at all; they were simply members of The Institutes staff, practitioners of the Doman-Delacato methods.

Doman and Delacato are Glenn J. Doman, over-all director of The Institutes; his brother Robert, the medical director; and Carl H. Delacato, then associate director of The Institutes and director of the Institute of Language Disability. We didn't meet the Domans and Delacato on our first day, but we did get introduced to a remarkable chart invented by them. It was called the Doman-Delacato Developmental Profile and is a model of normal neurological development. For hurt children it expresses a child's "neurological age" in visual form, by indicating the various levels at which his or her development has been blocked. Lying in St. Francis Hospital, Karen had had a neurological age of zero; now her language and her auditory understanding were quite good, but it was obvious she was going to rate low in mobility, manual competence, visual competence, and tactile competence. The object of The Institutes program, we were told, was to double or triple the rate of her neurological growth.

We stayed at The Institutes until ten that night and returned early the next morning feeling stimulated rather than tired, our adrenal glands apparently working overtime.

The evaluation continued. Karen was photographed a couple of times—an echoencephalogram (ultrasound) picture of the sound waves in her cranial cavity and a movie of her on a mat, as she was urged to demonstrate her highest form of mobility. She was seen by three doctors. We were told she was suffering "a severe alternating divergent strabismus"—her eyes were "looking" if not truly "seeing," but were not working together. And we were told by medical director Dr. Robert Doman, "Although there's no way of telling in advance which child will be helped, we would like very much to try Karen on the program.

"We haven't learned everything about the brain," he cautioned us, "but we think we can help Karen."

Most of the parents in our group were given similar encouragement—but not the teen-aged boy who had lunged for my sandwich. He was a moderately brain-injured boy who had been put into "special education" classes, was bright enough to perceive that he was more "different" than "special," and had gradually lapsed into psychosis. Now his mental problems overshadowed the physical problem of a hurt brain, and he simply wasn't competent to cope with the demands The Institutes program would have made on him.

As his parents led him to the family car, threatening to restrain him if he didn't behave himself, we felt a sense of pain, a terrible sorrow, yet, subconsciously at least, a sense of relief that he was gone. I'm sure none of us wanted to feel that our children shared that boy's problems. We didn't want to be reminded that our children might, years hence, be tortured by the same pressures, driven into the same dark chambers.

By the second day, we survivors of The Institutes' sorting-out process were being welded into a unit, and Barbara and I felt at ease enough to ask the parents of a lovely, raven-haired eight-year-old why they had brought their daughter here.

"Your daughter seems so . . . okay."

"She is, except for her left arm and hand."

We looked, but failed to see. "Her arm and hand?"

"She doesn't use them."

The raven-haired young lady under discussion was playing ball with a younger child at that moment, and we saw at once that her left arm was hanging limp. We wondered how both of us could have been so unobservant.

"She's been like that," her mother explained, "since an operation when her heart stopped beating briefly. She really manages pretty well now, without the left hand. It doesn't seem to bother her. But it will when she gets older, when she gets to high school, when she gets invited to dances. . . ."

The Luftwaffe captain's grasp of English was limited, but we learned that his four-year-old son, Johannes, had been seen and rejected by renowned clinics in several European cities. And Karen found a friend on the floor of the Evaluation Center— "the boy Rod," as she called him, from Grosse Point Park, Michigan.

The second day of evaluation was as long and hard as the first. And as we reported to The Institutes on the third morning, we said good-by to Karen. For two days, the children were to be evaluated without their parents while the parents were given a crash course in brain injury. Somewhat to our surprise, Karen left us willingly. She was thoroughly enjoying the games The Institutes staff had devised to test her skills and functions. When we gave her a kiss and said, "See you tonight," we realized it was the first time we had left her in the care of others, in the daytime, since bringing her home from the hospital five months before.

We were told to bring along jackets, even lap robes, and were led to a building near the main gate which housed a lecture hall. The temperature there was kept at sixty degrees, and strong lights shone down relentlessly on the student area. The cool air and bright lights were meant to keep us alert and receptive to a full-scale assault of facts, theories, ideas.

Glenn Doman—then in his late forties, his eyes narrowed, blue, penetrating—seemed as demanding and arbitrary as he was intensely knowledgeable and concerned. "There's a direct relationship," he told us, "between your understanding what we discuss here and your child's making it."

Several members of The Institutes staff lectured us in that two-day marathon brain briefing. We were given a short course on the physiology of the brain and a mind-battering series of lectures, workshop sessions, and just plain pep talks on IAHP methods and theories.

Reviewing my scribbled notes five years later, I find certain facts and theories emerging that seem even more vital to me today than when I first heard them.

The brain, my notes tell me, is tough.

Brain injury, they tell me, is vastly misunderstood by many medical men as well as by most laymen.

And God, they tell me, must be disappointed that we haven't learned to use our brains more effectively.

After living for more than five years with what brain injury means—and doesn't mean—I returned to my notes to sort the significant from the merely interesting. I found I could distill those two days of lecturing into a few pages:

The brain is the sturdiest, yet the most sensitive, of the vital organs. While it can survive terrible assaults and abuse, a seemingly minor injury to the brain can defy analysis and destroy a life. And the brain is impervious to pain; it directs all feeling yet has none of its own.

Brain-injured children are often wrongly classified as "mentally retarded." Children with one of the brain's two hemispheres removed surgically have been known to function at the level of genius, whereas even minor damage to the cortex—the area of the brain that controls thinking, voluntary functions—can in some cases mean severely impaired intellectual powers.[*]

Most brain-injured children have at one time or another had trouble using their two eyes together, say Doman-Delacato. Yet many youngsters categorized as "blind" simply haven't learned to see—just as thousands of youngsters tucked away in mental institutions as schizophrenic, or autistic, are brain-injured rather than mentally unbalanced, and could be helped.

Many people—even people who should know better—confuse the brain-injured child with the child born with a *deficient* brain. An improperly formed brain can't be rebuilt; a healthy but injured brain can, and the challenge is in finding ways for sending sensory messages to those millions of brain cells that *haven't* been impaired, in the areas of the brain that are failing to control functions as they should.

[*] My *Random House Dictionary of the English Language* declares: "Retardation. n. . . . 3. Slowness or limitation in intellectual understanding and awareness, emotional development, academic progress, etc." Note the "et cetera." Even the lexicographers are somewhat at a loss for words—for surely a child with impaired speech is in a sense "retarded." So is a child who finds it impossible to carry a tune, or accept affection. Many such shortcomings/defects/conditions/problems can, in fact, be caused by brain injury—and every human being is brain-injured to some degree. So mightn't we relegate "retarded," as a label for human beings, to some repository for inexact, obsolete, mindless, *needless* labels ("freak," "homo," "pinko," "illegitimate"), especially considering that there are strong differences of opinion as to what the word means or implies?

"A number of doctors have called us radicals," says Glenn Doman. "But the only radical thing we've ever said is that brain injury is in the brain. There are those who think we're leading a march away from medicine—when, in fact, we're leading a march *back* to medicine. We treat the disease, not the symptoms. We deal with brain injury, not the *results* of brain injury. When a man's right leg isn't following orders because his brain was hurt, does it make sense to send him to a right-leg doctor?"

The brain is very much like a computer, and if you increase the input, you increase the output. It's possible to speed up the development of the brain by speeding up the input—increasing the incoming stimuli in terms of frequency, intensity, and duration. When you fail to get output, something—an invisible shield—is blocking the cybernetic cycle. Sometimes this shield can be penetrated, and sometimes it can't, and no one seems to know why a technique works beautifully for one hurt child yet works not at all for another child with the same symptoms.

"Normal," in terms of brain development, merely means "average." Ordinary one-year-olds can be taught to read—so who's to say what normal is or should be?

There are three ways to treat/repair/influence the brain: surgically, chemically (vodka, ether, LSD), and physically, from the outside. The notion that you can't reach the brain from the outside—a notion seemingly held by many of those entrusted with the care of brain-injured children—is, argues the IAHP, a myth. You can't *not* reach the brain, The Institutes staff insists. We reach the brain every time we stimulate one of the senses.

"Stimulation"—that's the key word in reversing brain injury. Brain development is not a static situation; it's a dynamic, ever-changing process. The brain does most of its post-natal growing in the first 18 months of life, and is virtually completed when a child reaches the third grade or so. But brain *development,* in adults as well as children, can be slowed, or it can be speeded. The brain develops through *use.*

Conversely, the enemies of brain development are restriction, constriction, confinement, and their cousins. Playpens keep children where their mothers can keep an eye on them—but they also serve to limit the amount of learning (touching, seeing, tasting, smelling, listening) the child might be doing in the outside world. Playpens and solitary confinement deprive the brain of nutrition.

Man uses about 10 per cent of his brain cells, so he can afford to lose a lot of cells in a lifetime. The problem in restoring brain function is in finding new pathways to the unimpaired, unused brain cells.

A forceps injury at delivery? Prolonged high fever? A stroke? An aneurysm? Oxygen deprivation, such as Karen suffered? A bullet in the head? A mother who contracted German measles during pregnancy? . . . *How* a person comes to suffer brain injury has little or no bearing on whether the injury can be overcome. Brain injury is brain injury and should be diagnosed as such, not as spasticity or cerebral blindness or other *manifestations* of brain injury.

Proper crawling and creeping are essential steps in a child's neurological development. "Probably the most important thing we have ever found," say Doman and Delacato, "is the importance of putting kids on the floor. All other techniques fail if the child doesn't spend time on the floor." The simulated crawling known as "patterning" is a method of telling the brain what it feels like to move on the floor, a means of constant visual stimulation and a means of programming the brain by recapitulating nature.

"Until your child is well," we were told, "nobody in your family is going to be well. So don't tell us about the psychological problems of having a brain-injured child." Those problems won't go away until the physical problem—the problem in the brain—is solved. The basis of the problem is neurological, not psychological, and the solution is to increase neurological function, to make the child as independent as possible.

When the lecturing was over, at eight o'clock on a crisp wintery night, we walked through powdery snow that glistened in the moonlight, from the auditorium to the reception building where the children were gathered. We expected to find Karen weary and worn. Instead we found her bubbling with energy and enthusiasm. Obviously the day had been as stimulating for her as it had been for us, and her words came tumbling out in great, buoyant, vivid sentences as I lifted her to my shoulder.

"Daddy! I had a party, Daddy. I had ice cream! I had cake! . . . Mommy?"

Barbara, marvelling, reached out to her.

"I'm right here, Karen. Let's get your coat on. Did you know it had been snowing?"

"I had a party, Mommy!"

We said good night to the party-arrangers and went out into the parking lot. The snow had begun to fall again.

"I like snow," Karen said. Then, smacking her lips: "I taste the snow!"

"What does the snow taste like?" I asked.

She had to think about that one, and not until we got in the car and were on our way did she have her answer.

"It tastes like ice water, Daddy."

We drove through the snow that tasted like ice water to Nana and Grandpop's house, reviewed the day's activities over a pot of tea, and went to bed. The next day, Thursday, we returned to The Institutes for more lecturing. Friday was the final day of our evaluation week.

"These past two days," we were told, "you've heard the whys of brain injury. Today we're going to show you the hows—how you're going to help fix your child." And so Karen's first full-fledged "program" was prescribed for her, and it was thoroughly explained to us, for we were the ones who would have to carry it out.

First we were shown Karen's developmental profile, which the staff had prepared jointly. Her language skills—ability to speak and understand—were adjudged adequate for her age. Her mobility was hardly better than that of a newborn infant: she churned arms and legs without achieving any bodily movement. Her vision was no better than that of a two-month-old: her eyes reacted to strong light in a reflexive way, but she had little or no outline perception. As for her ability to differentiate objects by touch, she was merely slow for her age. But her manual competence was quite poor: she could wrap the fingers of one hand

—her right—around a small object at will, but couldn't make her fingers work together to achieve any higher function.

Karen's chronological age at the time was thirty-one months. Her neurological age—her functional age—measured considerably less than half that.

The Institutes staff was convinced that Barbara's undirected efforts at organizing a program of activities for Karen had been of enormous value, but they were going to ask us to work even harder, much harder, to narrow the gap, to speed up her rate of neurological growth, especially in the areas of mobility and vision. Barbara's eyes narrowed once or twice at the manner in which the instructions were presented ("Listen carefully, Mother, and write this just as I tell you. . . ."), but not at the work load itself.

We would have to build a new and larger patterning table, with a surface that was more tactilely stimulating, and we would be expected to increase the program to eight sessions a day, at five minutes per session. (Frequency. Intensity. Duration. These words were drilled into us.)

We were instructed in several patterning refinements—such as "brushing Karen's hands," to open her clenched fingers. It would be vital that Karen learn to crawl properly. Mastering this basic step in neurological development—crawling—would make higher functions that much easier for Karen to achieve. The old saying was sound: A child must (or should) creep before she can walk, crawl before she can creep. Should we skip a step, we could be assured of creating problems for her.

By putting Karen through her paces on a patterning table, we were, in effect, doing her crawling for her, sending sensory messages to her brain, establishing a pattern that the brain would eventually learn, so that it might send out the right signals to her hands, arms, and legs. Karen was not required to help at all. In fact, it would be best if she would simply relax and daydream while her patterning team manipulated her. If Karen *thought* about crawling and tried to help, she would be involving the cortex of the brain in the business of learning to crawl.

The cortex is meant to do our thinking, while other levels of the brain should be in charge of unconscious activities such as crawling and creeping. A child who has to *think* about crawling probably can't crawl and talk simultaneously.

When we had demonstrated that we were capable of instructing teams of volunteers in the fine art of patterning, we were summoned to learn our tactile program.

Elaine Lee—dark-haired, bespectacled, soft-spoken—was Karen's special friend on that initial visit to The Institutes. Miss Lee's loving, gently persuasive manner helped explain the attachment. So did the considerable and intriguing supply of miniature toys, buttons, and baubles tucked away in her desk drawers. But I'd like to think there was something beyond the toys and the personality that Karen responded to. It was the sense of discovery that those mini-toys promised, as Miss Lee placed them, one at a time, in Karen's palm.

"Here's one we've had before, Karen. Something special. Shall we see if that right hand of yours can tell me what it is?"

We hold our breath.

"The whistle?"

"Great, Karen. That's really good."

Miss Lee's toy therapy reinforced Karen's confidence that she could see things with her hands. She urged Karen forward with the technique a track-and-field coach might use in teaching a youngster how to high-jump. She was observing Karen's abilities, then raising the bar just enough to challenge a little girl without discouraging her.

Karen's tactile program was to consist of at least twelve minutes' work a day, divided into two short sessions so she would not lose interest. (Miss Lee subscribes to the show business dictum—alway leave them wanting more.) Karen's troublesome left hand—Lefty—was to work for seven minutes with hand-sized objects. Righty was to work for five minutes a day with smaller, dissimilar objects. Each object was to be explained and described carefully the first time it was presented. We were told to vary the objects frequently and to be willing to pause for a discussion any time Karen expressed an interest in an unfamiliar object or an unusually textured surface.

Lefty was to be given additional brushing over a variety of surfaces and objects. And bath time was to be utilized as an opportunity for tactile stimulation—rubbing her briskly with a washcloth, varying the bath temperatures, using a shower-spray hose if possible, and drying her vigorously with a rough towel.

"Roughhousing" and "pinching games" were prescribed, too. I got an A for effort for the "whee" games I had played—tossing Karen into the air—but even better, Miss Lee said, was a gentle tumble on the floor with her brother and sister.

After Miss Lee and the tactile program came the vision program.

Karen was cortically blind. She was not getting signals from her midbrain, via the optic nerves, to her two eyes. Her eyes appeared healthy; her pupils reacted reflexively to light. Yet more than six months after those moments of oxygen deprivation, she still had little or no ability to perceive the world around her through her eyes. She was *looking*, yet she couldn't see—and her eyes obviously weren't working together. Our neurologist's prediction that vision was the function least likely to be permanently impaired seemed sadly mistaken. The Institutes staff did suspect that she had some slight ability to perceive a dim outline of a well-lighted object—yet it was obvious that Karen wasn't using her eyes in any meaningful way.

We were to stimulate her eyes day and night. We would need a D-cell flashlight to dilate her pupils, a pencil flashlight which she was to be encouraged to follow in the dark, a string of Christmas lights—the winking kind—to be strung around her bed. I was also advised to write a letter to the Miller Brewing Company in Milwaukee, requesting one of their "color-in-motion sconces." These revolving cylinders, which produce an ever-changing spectrum of colors, no doubt were designed to hypnotize beer drinkers into ordering another Miller High Life. Might one also help penetrate the shield blocking Karen's vision, at least enough to draw her to it? Karen was to spend much of her free time heading downhill on her slide, with the beer-company beacon at the bottom, as an inducement to move forward.

The slide I had built the previous summer was inadequate. I was to build a new one—longer, wider, adjustable to a range of heights. When not on her slide, Karen was to be on the floor, on her tummy.

Even in her sleep Karen was to be encouraged to assume a position such as she would be in if she were crawling. One night she was to be placed on her stomach with her left arm and knee pointing up, her head turned toward her left hand and the hand in the sucking position, and the right arm and leg extended straight down. On alternate nights this position—"the sleep position," in IAHP vernacular—was to be reversed. We were to place Karen in a sleep position at her bedtime and to check the position again just before we went to bed.

"Masking" was to be done at least twelve times a day, for precisely sixty seconds each time, with an interval of at least half an hour between maskings. We were given three plastic masks, with the red figure of a spaceman emblazoned on each, to cover Karen's nose, mouth and chin. "Space masks" we called them, and they caused Karen to rebreathe the carbon dioxide she exhaled, thus helping her to breathe more deeply, ultimately feeding a richer supply of oxygen to her brain and perhaps helping prevent seizures.

We were charged a dollar apiece for the masks and given a set of plans for the slide. In the months ahead we would be asked to construct an assortment of unheard-of devices prescribed for "Karen's program," and we often thought of the time and energy we might have saved had The Institutes contracted with someone in Philadelphia to make these devices to order. We wondered aloud why this couldn't be arranged and were told, "We get enough flak from organized medicine, without having them accuse us of prescribing programs so we can sell equipment."

Finally, The Institutes staff agreed, Karen should be on a restricted diet—low in sugar and salt and high in meat, cheese, eggs, and vegetables. Her fluid intake was not to exceed twenty ounces a day—and fluid was interpreted as "anything that spills or melts in the mouth." On her prohibited list were thirst-producers such as potato chips, popcorn, and peanut butter* and almost any desserts other than fruits, custards, and plain wafers.

Most important was the restriction on liquid intake. Fluids, we were told, can be one of the brain's worst enemies. A proportion of the fluid you pour into your body inevitably finds its way to the brain. Your skull can't expand, so if you increase the volume of fluids in the brain, you crowd the blood vessels and reduce the volume of blood needed to feed the brain. Too much fluid decreases the brain's efficiency, and Karen couldn't afford any loss of efficiency.

"There's no need to fill the tank every time Karen is thirsty," we were told. "Give her a one- or two-ounce drink instead of an eight-ounce glass."

Mask, slide, diet, flashlights, patterning table, assorted tactile activities—Karen's program was going to be a full-time job, to make up for lost time, to speed up her neurological growth rate.

"All we have to offer," Glenn Doman tells everyone who makes the pilgrimage to Stenton Avenue, "is an unreasonable program which sometimes works"—an unreasonable program which "unleashes the power of parents."

The program already seemed to be having an unreasonably cohesive effect on the families who had gone through evaluation week with us. By week's end a bond had been established between us, and we drew strength from one another, from our shared experiences with hurt brains, from our common hopes and prayers, and from the intense, exhilarating days we had just been through together.

The mother of Karen's friend—"the boy Rod," now lying limp on the floor—showed us a snapshot of the son she had had before he was stricken.

We exchanged addresses with the parents of Victor, who was

---

* Two years later, the IAHP would shift gears and *prescribe* peanut butter—"natural" peanut butter—because of its low salt and high protein value.

fed through a tube, and with the Luftwaffe captain, the farmer from Missouri, the osteopath from central Pennsylvania, and with others from Wisconsin, New Jersey, New York, Michigan, Ohio, and Utah.

We found kindred spirits in a family from just outside Cincinnati. Their Leslie was about the age of our Karen, and she, too, had been born "normal." An attack of encephalitis, and its resultant high fever, had knocked her for a loop when she was an infant—"She came home from the hospital a different person," said her mother—yet her parents' apprehension about her slow development after her illness had been shrugged off by the family pediatrician. "She'll be fine," he said, and he found nothing disturbing in Leslie's peculiar choice of snacks—pickles, peppery foods, and soap cakes.

Leslie was a few months older than Karen when we met, and although she seemed a happy child, she obviously had problems. She crawled on her hands and knees but could not stand on her feet, and her almost constant knuckle-chewing was a way of telling us she had virtually lost her sense of taste.

Suddenly it was time to say good-by to Leslie and "the boy Rod" and Miss Lee and the rest of The Institutes staff. The parents wished one another well, the staff asked us if we had any final questions ("Don't leave," we were instructed, "until every one of your questions has been answered"), and I was called into an office marked "Administrator." Because I had given my occupation as journalist, and had been observed making occasional notes during the lectures, The Institutes' administrator felt obliged to offer me a piece of advice.

"Do us a favor," she said. "Don't write a book about Karen. Just make her better."

I explained my long-time addiction to note-taking, but declared I was not a book writer and had no notion of authoring a book about Karen.

"That's good," I was told, "because every time The Institutes is written up, another flood of letters pour in, and our waiting list gets that much longer. We hate to get more people's hopes up, and then have to tell them that we can't see them for at least two years."*

Driving back from The Institutes to Nana and Grandpop's for the last time that week, we were raring to get started on Karen's vastly expanded and reshaped program. We couldn't imagine how we were going to accomplish everything The Institutes was asking of us and have time left for such luxuries as grocery shopping and snow shoveling, but we had high hopes that our efforts would pay off and that this carefully prescribed program of activities would put Karen on the road to recovery.

The road we had been following up until our visit had been a winding road, it now seemed. We had been heading in the right general direction, but we were traveling slowly, over unfamiliar terrain, via back roads where we were unable to recognize many of the landmarks.

Now, at last, we were getting a set of instructions from some people who seemed to know the way. They told us, in effect, that if we shifted into high gear and followed their map, we had a better chance of reaching our destination, and of reaching it sooner.

* The Institutes has since modified this position, as explained later.

CHAPTER VI

Rare Gifts

Music belongs near the top of the list of skills for which no one in our family has demonstrated any genius. I can't gap a spark plug or tread water; Barbara is unable to deal with people over the telephone or open olive jars and will never learn the difference between a comma and a semicolon. But the world of music is one area where our non-talents seem perfectly matched.

Yet music proved particularly helpful to us in carrying out Karen's intensive program when we returned home from The Institutes on the first day of December 1966.

We had been apprehensive, before going to Philadelphia, that we were going to be required to take music out of Karen's life, having heard that this sacrifice was part of the regimen for children who were "on the program." But we had been misled. Brain-injured youngsters who are at that stage of development when they should be establishing "laterality"—enforcing a pattern of either right- or left-handedness—can be subconsciously confused by music, we were told when we got to the IAHP. The dominant hemisphere of our brain, be it left or right, is in charge of our communications skills, while the opposite side looks after tonal qualities; so it happens that some aphasic kids and stutterers who have not established dominance and can scarcely say their names are able to sing, having learned songs through the tonal qualities rather than the words. Because music is less demanding than language for most children to learn, the brain is apt to accept musical stimulation while depressing other kinds of stimulation it is receiving simultaneously. Music, therefore, can confuse a child who is trying to establish dominance. Karen might, it was felt, face a dominance crisis a couple of years hence, but she wasn't at that advanced a stage yet and she was welcome in the meantime to lavish her affection on "Puff the Magic Dragon" and "Burl Ives Sings 'The Little White Duck' and Other Children's Favorites."

The baby grand piano at the home of Larry and Flo D'Aleo had proved a great hit with Karen when she was introduced to it one late summer evening before her evaluation at The Institutes. She was overjoyed to discover that her Righty could produce such splendid sounds on what she called "the meo" and had invited herself back to the D'Aleos' on numerous occasions. We decided a toy piano for Karen and a xylophone for Gretchen should head the girls' lists for Santa that year. But in the meantime, during the last month of 1967, Karen insisted on records and meo music. Barbara found herself called upon to direct eight *a cappella* musical interludes daily— one for each and every patterning session.

Karen had always enjoyed musical accompaniment with her patterning, but now she was virtually telling us that if we expected her to get up on that table eight times a day we would be expected to make the whole thing a bit more entertaining. Over the next few months, the adult trios gathered around our patterning table must have sung "Happy Birthday to You" to just about every one of the 42,000 residents of the town of Enfield, and "Are You Sleeping, Brother John?" became "Are You Sleeping, Sister Gretchen? . . . Father Bill? . . . Mother Barbara?" ad infinitum.

Finding volunteers for eight patterning sessions per day, every day of the week, was a difficult enough task in itself without insisting on accomplished singers, but patterning organizer Gail Ellis did, in fact, manage to assemble quite a few tuneful groups.

Gail had been a close friend of Barbara's at Penn State, and we had spent a few nights on Gail and Rob's sofa bed in Windsor Locks, upon our arrival in Connecticut, when John was on the way and Karen had not yet been contemplated. We also had joined the Ellises' church, First Presbyterian of Enfield, and as soon as we returned from The Institutes Gail appeared at our kitchen door volunteering to organize some church women into patterning teams for us. She and a church friend canvassed the women of First Presbyterian, and Gail contacted other friends of ours who had worked with Karen before Philadelphia, or had said they would like to, and assigned one or more regular times and days to each of the volunteers. Barbara herself was a part of all but a couple of the sessions. If someone found she would have to miss a session, she was to phone Gail, who would find a substitute.

I was to serve as a one-man emergency team. By that time I was spending most of my working hours in a second-floor office directly above the patterning room, contemplating the wallpaper and having a go at free-lance writing. I had a private phone in my office, but Barbara saw no need to tie up two telephone lines every time one of our "patterning ladies" failed to show up; she simply tapped on the exposed pipe connecting my radiator and the one on the floor below. Three short taps meant "I'm sorry to interrupt you in the middle of a paragraph, but please come right down and give us a hand."

I was not, however, the only male involved in the program. Rob Ellis came on Sunday mornings, right after dropping his kids off at Sunday school; the superintendent of the Sunday school gave up every Sunday afternoon; and a sixteen-year-old named Tommy volunteered for Saturday afternoons. Most of the other time slots were filled by Flo, Betty, Phyllis, Marion, Toni, Mary Jo, Sheila, Dolly, Ellerslie, Lin, Peg, Betty, Connie, Jean, Brenda, Cindy, Ethel, Irene, Alice, Sally, Nancy, Judy, Emmalou, Joanne, Gwen, Frances, two Dotties, two Dianes, and three novices from Our Lady of the Angels Convent—Marie, Linda and Maryann.

Karen's response to her accelerated program was all we could have hoped for. By mid-December her eyes were able to follow flashlight movements in the dark, both vertically and horizontally. And within a couple of days of that achievement she dem-

onstrated that some of her patterning "input" was finding its
way out.

The payoff came just before Christmas, after an investment
of close to a thousand patterning sessions, plus a few weeks'
worth of assistive-crawling effort.

Following our Philadelphia visit the month before, an assistive-crawling session had been incorporated into each patterning
period. Karen was put on the floor in the crawl position. One of
us would brace a hand against the foot of whichever leg was
flexed. Then we would encourage Karen—with a slight pinch if
necessary—to push against the braced hand.

At first, these efforts seemed only to have helped her move
her arms and legs more freely, and although we had seen a
sense of desire quickening within her, her efforts still hadn't
progressed much beyond arm-flailing.

But at Christmastime, she began to push against a hand when
we pinched her, and within a few days she turned her head and
cocked the other leg, so that with a few more pinches and words
of encouragement she was moving herself forward. She had, in
effect, begun to crawl.

Word of this breakthrough spread rapidly through our world
of patterners, and when Sally Masters's patterning day rolled
around—the Sally Masters who had been a fellow patient at
St. Francis—the entire Masters family came along to witness
Karen's achievement.

Sally was speechless over Karen's demonstration of her newfound ability to move.

"Thank you, Sally," said Barbara, after the applause for
Karen had subsided. "And Merry Christmas."

"Thank me?" said Sally in amazement. "I should thank you.
Karen's crawling was the most thrilling Christmas present I
could ask for."

Another Sally—Sally Streibig, of Philadelphia—and young
Billy Kirchmeier, Käthe's brother, were responsible for that
year's grandest gifts under our tree.

Sally and Ralph Streibig had been the closest of friends during our Philadelphia years, before we moved to Connecticut to build a newspaper and a family. We had drunk champagne at one another's wedding. We had shivered together at the Mummer's Parade and popped popcorn together at the fireplace of the former wheelwright's shop which was our Bryn Athyn home, and Barbara had tended baby Karla Streibig several days a week while Sally taught school and Ralph became a student again. Now our families were four hundred miles apart, and Karen needed help.

The Streibigs' gift was made of scraps and love. Ralph had prevailed upon a local lumberyard operator to part with a dozen 6 by 16″ samples of prefinished paneling, and Sally had fashioned these into a handsome and highly imaginative set of "tactile boards" for a little girl, now thirty-two months of age, who could do nothing for herself and who still had trouble distinguishing between a block and a ball. A few of the boards had strips of variously textured materials—ranging from sandpaper and wool to plastic and silk—affixed to them. Karen was to learn to identify these by touch. The remainder of the boards were to help the Karen of tomorrow. A big zipper, a little zipper, sets of king-sized snaps and hooks, a silver-dollar-sized button—all set in brightly patterned corduroys, nylons and polished cottons, and mounted on boards, to hasten the day when Karen could master the skills necessary to dress herself.

Seven-year-old Billy Kirchmeier, too, was looking ahead that Christmas, and his vision was enough to make our eyes blur with emotion. The youngest of the seven Kirchmeier children, Billy was rewarded not with money, but with supermarket trading stamps for chores well performed. He had squirreled away his stamp books against the day when he saw something he really wanted, and during a pre-Christmas trip to the stamp-redemption center he found a premium worthy of his months of hoarding—a Karen-sized rocking chair.

We said our "Thank you, Billy" with more than a little gratitude, partly because of Billy's sacrifice, but mostly because a seven-year-old boy knew that Karen, who had to be lifted onto the chair and told not to be afraid, would one day be able to manage a rocking chair by herself.

"Merry" was not precisely the right word for that holiday period, but we were indeed merrier than we had been for months, and it would be difficult to imagine a more meaningful Christmas. On Christmas Eve "baby Gretchen," aged thirteen months, was given a precious gift which Karen had possessed for only twelve short months: She rose to her feet and walked. John, aged four, exchanged home-baked cakes with his very good next-door friend—Emma Stewart, aged ninety-one. Nana and Grandpop drove up from Philadelphia, with the trunk of their old T-bird weighted down with surprises, and with the determination to give Barbara some much-needed relief in the patterning and kitchen-work departments. And on the Sunday after Christmas our patterning trio of Our Lady of the Angels novices serenaded Karen and the rest of us in our living room by playing what seemed to be the entire score from *The Sound of Music* on Karen's toy piano.

Our 1967 Christmas card was displayed on northern Connecticut mantlepieces and sideboards long after the tree lights and toy trains had been packed away, our friends told us. I had made three individual photographs of the children—a smiling John, seated with book; Gretchen of the double chin, seated with stuffed Santa; an alert-looking Karen on her tummy, head raised, right hand grasping a clutch ball. The photos were silhouetted and affixed to a piece of posterboard which Barbara dressed up with sketches of pine boughs and tree ornaments, and the completed work of art was taken to a printing shop and reproduced in greeting-card size. Close friends who knew of Karen's brush with death were elated by this cheerful likeness of her, and faraway friends who hadn't heard about her illness couldn't have suspected her problems from that photo, didn't have to be told what we had gone through that year.

Soon after Christmas we worked out a way to reduce the number of patterners—and patterners' children—trooping through the kitchen to the playroom.

During the earliest days on The Institutes program, Barbara had felt obliged to offer a cup of coffee, at the very least, to these women who were giving so willingly of their time and energies. But entertaining takes its toll, and when the over-all strain began to tell, coffee became a do-it-yourself project and team organizer Gail rearranged the schedule so that two teams a day would come for an entire hour, replacing four teams who stayed for fifteen minutes. These two teams were to stay for two patterning-table sessions each, and to use the fifty minutes between sessions to accomplish a great many of the other activities on Karen's program.

Barbara thereby was granted a couple of Karen-free hours to tend to housekeeping, John and Gretchen. I took John to nursery school in the mornings. Gretchen had Barbara to herself during Karen's solid hour of programming and delighted in helping make the beds. It was a treat for Gretchen when the patterning ladies brought little friends for her to play with—and a bit of a wrench for Barbara when Gretchen used her newfound skill at walking to fetch a cookie for her big sister, just as Karen had run to bring a diaper or rattle for "baby Gretchie" not so many months before.

"I often think," Barbara said not long ago, "that Gretchen grew up by herself." No complaints, really—just a statement of fact. The Institutes would have approved of the fact that we were too busy at that period in Gretchen's life to restrict her freedom, her tendency to explore things, and that we didn't nag her to "stop crawling and stand on your feet" simply because she had learned to walk. We were grateful, in fact, to have her nearby as a model of creeping and crawling, while we groped for ways of encouraging the same skills in Karen.

John, meanwhile, was forever begging permission to bring a friend home from nursery school or to visit another youngster's house. Barbara thought at the time that he was overly anxious to have playmates outside the family, perhaps to make up for something he was missing, but these motherly fears were unwarranted, she later decided, when Karen and Gretchen displayed the same insistent need as they approached the age of five. (Echo from The Institutes: "You don't have a psychological problem, Mother—you have a physical problem, in your child's brain.")

Karen, who had been toilet-trained well before her brain injury—but not since—had her first successful "potty" experience during that Christmas season, and during the first week in January Barbara had a premonition of further achievement. After three successive nights of concern over Karen's sleeplessness—we had difficulty getting her to sleep, and she would awaken two or three times each night, crying each time—Barbara declared, "She's on the verge of something."

And she was. I brought Karen to our bed on the morning of Saturday, January 6, and as the sunlight streamed through the bay window, I silently raised one of my hands, held it between the sun and Karen's eyes, and wiggled my fingers. Karen lay still but intent for a moment, then asked, "What's Daddy doing? . . . I want the flashlight."

Until that moment, it seemed she had been able to see nothing other than a flashlight's beam in a darkened room. Was she now perceiving that I had somehow blocked the sun's warmth —or had her eyes detected the motion of my hand? We couldn't be certain at the time, but we willingly grasped at any evidence of returning vision. I now suspect that Barbara's intuition was right, that Karen's wakefulness was indeed caused by her being "on the verge of something"—on the verge of visual perception.

(Not until several months later did we discover another extraordinary loss of function Karen had suffered: She was—and still is—unable to close her eyes voluntarily. Her eyes close reflexively when she's threatened or weary, but she cannot say to herself, "Eyes—close!" So when she awakens in the wee hours, she is unable to shut out the strange sights and shadows of night simply by closing her eyes. She has therefore been more inclined than most children to cry when she awakens—demanding nothing really, just expressing momentary fear until she receives a word of comfort or until sleep overtakes her once again. The waking and crying began in that first week of 1968, and so, we suspect, did the return of meaningful vision.)

In the weeks that followed, the only other evidence that one or both of her two good eyes were beginning to get stronger signals from her brain was her ability to follow a large, slowly moving red flashlight in a darkened room. She continued unable to follow a pencil flashlight even in total darkness.

Obviously responding to the attention and concern being lavished upon her, Karen began growing up emotionally and socially as well as physically. Within two months she recognized all of her patterners, if not by voice then by some other trait. And she made a first effort at singing along at patterning time—no melody but fragments of lyrics. "Rock-a-bye Baby" came out "Rock-a-baby . . . wind blows . . . baby come down."

"Kan," she called herself, and it was fine to wake up to the early morning chirping we began to hear from her room:

"Why Kan wake up?" Pause, then words from a favorite song. "This old man come rolling home."

By the end of January she was able to sit up "all by self" on the newly tiled playroom floor we had laid for her. She would lose her balance easily and tumble sideways or backward, but the very fact that she could sit made her a better playmate for some of the little girls who trailed their mothers into our home at patterning time. A three-year-old chatterbox named Sandy seemed to love gabbing with Karen. And Brenda Masters, daughter of Sally, would sit opposite Karen on the floor, spread-legged, and offer to play ball. What Brenda had in mind was pushing Karen's clutch ball back and forth, but Karen, when she managed to find the ball with her good right hand, was inclined to cling to it.

"Don't you *want* to play with me?" Brenda would ask, puzzled but determined.

There were occasional days of unexplained stubbornness and willfulness, when Karen would throw aside tactile toys that were handed her for identification, and cry, or lie still and silent, when we tried to stimulate her to do some assistive crawling after a patterning session. We surmised that she might simply be wearying of the game and were glad when it was time, in February, to return to 8801 Stenton Avenue to recharge our batteries.

We brought with us to Philadelphia an encouraging report from our pediatrician, who had ordered another electroencephalogram test and had reported that while abnormal brain waves remained widespread—making Karen's damage difficult to pinpoint—the results indicated great general improvement.

"Fantastic!" was the reaction of The Institutes' Sandy Brown, not to the EEG report, but to her discovery that Karen was able to follow a flashlight vertically, with her right eye at least. "A very significant step," said Sandy. Most children who are visually at Level II on the Doman-Delacato Developmental Profile —meaning they have outline perception but no appreciation of detail—can see left-to-right movement of light but not up-and-down movement.

Sandy was delighted to detect in Karen's right hand the beginnings of cortical opposition—not merely grasping with the whole hand but the ability to command thumb and finger together to perform some task. Karen also demonstrated improved sitting balance. She showed great improvement in her ability to identify textures and objects by touch, and she was able to show off the kind of pinch-and-push crawling she had demonstrated for Sally Masters at Christmastime.

The emphasis over the next couple of months was to be on mobility and vision. We could cut down the number of patterning sessions from eight a day to six, but these were to be increased to seven minutes in length and supplemented with a sixty-second "swimming" session to precede each patterning.

This "swimming" was to be accomplished on an inclined board placed atop the patterning table, so that we could move Karen's hands and arms *under* her body, as she would if she were actually swimming or crawling. "Swimming," we were told, would also develop her ability to use her fingers for turning, twisting, pouring.

We were given instructions in building a swimming board and in administering a daily, pre-breakfast "salt-glo" treatment. This task was to be her father's province and consisted of giving her stubbornly rigid left arm and hand some straightforward physical therapy—a massage with a salt paste coarse enough to "pink" the arm, followed by warm rinse, cool rinse, rubdown with coarse towel, alcohol rub and lotion.

Mealtime—and even story time—was to be used more constructively. We could pass cookies to her left hand and offer smaller pieces of food such as dried fruit to her Righty. We were to encourage her auditory competence by telling her short stories, then asking questions that would lead her to relate the story back to us in a sequential manner.

The need for more time on her slide, said an M.D. on The Institutes staff, was very much indicated. Karen should spend a couple of hours a day on the slide and should be given four to six assistive-crawling sessions daily—not aimless crawling, but crawling in the direction of a "light box" we were to build so that she would be motivated toward interesting silhouettes placed against a brightly lit backdrop. I was also to build a light board with sockets for four 25-watt bulbs—red, blue, yellow and green—each controlled by its own pull chain.

To discourage her from rocking over from her stomach onto her back while on the floor I was to construct a three-legged aluminum frame to keep Karen face down, with a piece of belting riveted to the frame and strapped around Karen so that she could not escape from it. We were certain Karen would hate this device.

Two of the youngsters who had been through our evaluation period with us were back for their first re-evaluation on the day that we returned with Karen—and we were heartened by what we saw. Little Victor—undersized, fed through a tube, and unable even to turn his head ten weeks previous—was now taking food from a jar, gaining weight, and crawling like a young man with a mission. And Jimmy, the osteopath's son who could walk but was suffering from a host of other problems, was responding well to a program that kept him on his hands and knees for much of the day.

We said good-by once again, more encouraged than ever, were told to keep up the good work, and were given an appointment for mid-May.

"We have good luck with these amblyopic kids" were the parting words of Dr. Evan Thomas, whose mock-serious, grand-fatherly manner delighted Karen. His words cheered us, even though I couldn't find "amblyopic" in my desk dictionary. (It means, we've since learned, dimness of vision for no organic reason.)

En route back to Connecticut from The Institutes, Karen was in fine humor and seemed raring to go to work on "my new program." As we headed north on the Merritt Parkway, we tuned in a news broadcast on our car radio and rode on in silence as the news was followed by soft music.

"I hear the mickets," Karen announced eventually.

Barbara corrected her. *"Music, Karen. Say mu."*

"Mu," said Karen.

"Good. Now say *zick*."

"Zick."

"Fine, Karen. Now . . . '*mu-zick*.'"

"Mickets."

Karen was also getting language lessons from her brother, and shortly after her return to Enfield she adopted what seemed his favorite expression at the time—"Oh no!"

Karen's near domination of center stage was a bit hard for four-year-old John to take, and even though friends went out of their way to include him in special events, he let us know that he felt somewhat neglected, especially during patterning time, when his behavior left quite a lot to be desired.

Discussing this IAHP-aggravated version of the sibling-rivalry syndrome with another mother at The Institutes, Barbara had been told, "I heard of one youngster who crawls into the fireplace to play every time his sister is patterned." That sort of inspirational tale we didn't need.

"Where's the fireplace?" were the first words we heard from Karen's room one Sunday morning in early March. We had sat around the fireplace the night before and had sensed that Karen saw the firelight better than ever.

The color red seemed to be registering on her consciousness. We had had success with the red flashlight and with the red light on the light board Grandpop and I had built. Karen needed no urging to "do my lights" with her light board, Gretchen pulling the chains (until Karen was able) and Karen attempting to identify the colors. She was consistently right on red, but at first she merely guessed at the others.

Karen loved her early morning "salt rub" and was soon issuing instructions on what step I should take—"Next the towel . . . next alcohol." And much to our surprise, she didn't rebel at the aluminum frame that kept her face down on the floor.

When she had done good work, I rewarded her by taking her along on my morning jaunt to our neighborhood post office. If the sidewalks were clear, she was propped up in John's stake wagon. If there was a blanket of white on the ground, and John was home, she sat between her brother's legs on his sled and enjoyed her tumbles in the snow as much as any youngster.

As the woolly skies of winter began to roll back in late March, Karen got a jump on springtime.

Her slide was by the wall that the dining room shared with the kitchen. To get from slide to kitchen, she had only to advance two feet and turn left. Those had seemed an awfully long two feet, but toward the end of March her patterning and "swimming" program began to pay off. Her co-ordination finally caught up with her vitality, and she managed to inch her way down the slide and into the kitchen, without our helping hands but with encouraging shouts of "Push, Karen! Push!"

When the trio from Our Lady of the Angels ("the Girls" was Karen's collective name for them) came for their Sunday afternoon program, they not only encouraged a repeat performance but helped Karen double her speed.

"She's doing all the work with her legs," one of the Girls observed. "Maybe if we told her to 'swim' rather than 'push,' she would use her hands." And she did.

On Monday, April 1, we knew spring had come for Karen.

After her 1 P.M. patterning session she was put on the playroom floor for assistive crawling. I had been summoned to lend a hand at that session, but, of course, no one had had a clue that history was about to be made. Karen made her way across the playroom floor, pushing one foot and then the other against her mother's hand.

Suddenly she stopped. Her face was about a foot and a half from a little cedar bucket containing a ten-inch artificial geranium plant—a craft-shop souvenir we had brought back from a Vermont holiday when Karen was four months old and which we had utilized as part of her visual and tactile program. Barbara had spent many an hour with Karen by the west window of the playroom, urging her to touch, to "see" various red objects—the red ball, the red Santa, the red geranium—but she seemed to have made no progress. Now the geranium sat quite alone on the floor, bathed in a strong shaft of sunlight. Karen had not touched its blossoms that day, and no one had mentioned them; so we were not at all prepared for her historic announcement:

"I see the flowers!"

Pandemonium.

As our cheers subsided and as seven-year-old Jamie Descy stopped leaping for joy, Karen smiled and made a modest request: "Kiss for dat!"

Karen's father and our cold-nosed schnauzer, Doktor Pfeffer, were the first to oblige her.

CHAPTER VII

John

The Day Karen Saw the Geraniums was a milestone in our lives, holding out promise that Karen was to be liberated from cortical blindness, and that those who loved her were to be liberated from unspoken fears.

The return of meaningful vision would be a long and often baffling process, but we had witnessed a beginning and had no reason to believe that her progress would level off. We couldn't relax our efforts, but we might allow ourselves a larger measure of what we had once considered "normal" living.

Over the weeks that followed, we perceived more evidence of returning vision. The fresh evidence did not come as dramatically as "I see the flowers!"—but it did serve to reinforce our growing optimism. One day Karen saw the outline of a hand bathed in the beam of a flashlight, and reached out to touch it. Another day she found the image of a flower on the playroom wallpaper—again with the help of a flashlight.

Yet she continued to "see" things with her hands; finding them with her eyes was usually termed (by Karen) "peeking."

"What's this, Karen?" she was asked at bedtime when confronted with a favorite toy she had previously been able to identify only by touch.

"The puppy?" she answered uncertainly.

"Right! . . . Which puppy, Karen?"

"The blue puppy!"

"Wonderful, Karen." Pause for hug and kisses. "And what's this?"

"The dolly."

"No, Karen. Peek again."

"The pussycat?"

"Great, Karen. That was just great."

"I wanna do more peeking."

On Easter Karen was presented a ceramic bunny baked and glazed by N. Bartolotta of the Enfield Police Department. Her third birthday, April 27, 1968, was celebrated with the traditional ice cream and cake, and Karen seemed more interested in candles than anything else (candles which glowed and flickered—excellent for "peeking"). Her birthday party was a modest but happy affair, with just one bittersweet moment, as Karen sat in her high chair, slightly bewildered, while half a dozen other children raced around the room whirling their noisemakers. (The act of sitting in the high chair, with balance so greatly improved since her hospitalization, was a victory in itself.)

The day after her birthday was a Sunday, so we declared half a day's holiday from patterning and drove out to West Granby, Connecticut, to inspect what John had always referred to as "the tiny house in the woods," or simply "the Tiny House"—a cabin we had bought while living atop the *Press* and which had been almost totally neglected since Karen's hospitalization. Karen "peeked" her orange juice for the first time that morning, and when I held her out over the bubbling brook behind our cabin, so that she—following her brother's example—might make a splash with a stone and feel the swift and chilling current race between her fingers, she squealed, "I see the water!"

John was overjoyed to be returning to the Tiny House, where he had celebrated his third birthday, caught his first fish, toasted his first marshmallow, set out on his first "exploring" adventure. John and I determined to return soon to tend to some much-needed general maintenance and to feed a few more worms to a few more trout.

James Kealey, feisty friend of John Breisky's, accompanied

us on that return visit, and the back seat conversation soon deteriorated into a muted mumbling of some newly learned and impolite small-boy expressions. I was just beginning to get the drift of the conversation when I heard John giggle and say, "Dog-do."

I summoned a reproachful expression and uttered a single word of censure—"John!?"

The reply I received was both unhesitating and unconvincing: "I didn't say dog-do."

John caught a fine trout that day.

We needed John that spring and summer as much as he needed us. We needed his five-year-old vision of the world around us and his example of how healthy children respond to the sights and sounds of life. We rejoiced in his vitality and in his small-child wonderings and wanderings. Because of Karen, John received a smaller portion of our time and energies than he deserved, but the special times we did spend together became more meaningful, as he demonstrated for us many of the skills and traits we might help Karen achieve.

John was and is a lover of nature's bounties. In the weeks following our reunion with the Tiny House he helped me tend my cultivated dandelions and was a willing and interested guinea pig in an experiment to determine whether dandelion milk really does remove warts. (It doesn't.) He designed a domicile for ladybugs in one of our apple trees and christened it the Ladybug Club. And one day he appeared in the doorway to my office to announce, "The Indians made pictures with berry ink. Can I do it, too?"

I gave him my blessing, so he plucked a feather from an Indian war bonnet in his toy chest and asked me to fashion a quill pen. Then he gathered some wild berries and squooshed them into a pasty "ink." I still have a specimen of his Indian art.

Our major springtime outing—a rare day off from "the program"—was a trip to the Bronx Zoo on the New Haven Railroad's "Zoo Train," which left the Thompsonville station at 7:47 A.M. and made stops in Windsor Locks ("Why can't we be at the zoo now, Daddy?"), Hartford ("Why is all that smoke coming up from under these train cars?"), Meriden ("I want to see the aminals!"), said Milford ("Is this where the train gets gasoline?").

Informed that our train had only two engines and that they were off-limits to almost-five-year-olds, John announced, "You know what kind of train I'm going to run when I grow up? Just a lot of engines, and all the children will get to ride in them."

A sign on one cage at the zoo said, "White-Tailed Gnu," but our son knew better. "I think," said John, "he's a buffalo in front and a horse in back." No college zoology book will give you a better definition of a white-tailed gnu than that.

And after watching in awe as a red-haired, long-armed simian from Sumatra hoisted a fifteen-foot log, swung by his toes, then performed an incredible succession of acrobatic feats, John wondered, "Can *you* do that, Daddy?"

John was our pattern of childhood, a measuring standard for behavior, a link to adventure, for us and for Karen.

He was glad to provide the evening "roughhousing" that had been prescribed for Karen. He remained somewhat baffled by her loss of function, however, and the interests he shared with his sister had diminished considerably since her illness. It was often difficult for him to summon the patience to play at her speed. But he did treat her as his little sister, occasionally a pal and occasionally a pest. His responses to her were honest, never patronizing.

John set an example of resourcefulness and self-reliance. Karen admired her brother's ability to look after himself, and she soon learned to say "Be quiet, Johnny" if he interrupted her at dinnertime. She tuned in on his conversations with friends and would try to emulate him, making declarations such as "I'm gonna play baseball with the kids," without having any comprehension of what "baseball" meant.

John was required to apologize for bad behavior, and while

it was difficult to impose precisely the same standards on Karen (she was, after all, younger—and might she withdraw into a shell, begin to question her own worth, if we had to correct her behavior as well as her ability to crawl and hold a spoon?), we tried to make her feel she was a member of the family who must tow the line, not a special character.

Late one afternoon, John, Karen and Gretchen were in the tub together, having a rub-dub-dub of a time, when Karen accidentally kicked John. I asked her to apologize but could get no response at all.

At dinner she sat with head drooped over her dish as I spooned rhubarb pudding into her mouth, and again it was my task to remonstrate.

"Can't you raise your head, Karen?"

"I eat like dis" was her reply.

When I explained that "puppies eat that way, because they don't have fingers—just feet," her head came up, but again she muttered not a word.

At bedtime that night Barbara received the apology that I had requested: "I'm sorry I kicked my brother."

She also received confirmation that Karen had absorbed my lesson in canine anatomy: "Docky [Doktor Pfeffer] doesn't have any fingers!"

We knew that Karen was learning a great deal from her big brother, as well as from her parents. And it was becoming more and more apparent that she was beginning to teach *us* a few lessons, in courage and determination.

CHAPTER VIII

Geraldine

I'm ashamed to say that I can't recall the precise birth date of our fourth child, Geraldine. It was a Saturday, though—I'm certain of that, because Saturday was the day when Sheila Kealey, mother of Jimmy and of our summer helper, Diane, always came to spend the morning with Karen.

Sheila parked her old Chevvy wagon in our driveway that sunny summer morning, climbed the steps to the back porch, crossed the porch, opened the screen door, surveyed the scene, stepped inside as she uttered a cheerful "Hi, Barb," then winked and asked, like some Dublin version of Sherlock Holmes, "And where is Karen?"

Karen, in full view on the floor, between refrigerator and sink, joined in the fun immediately: "She's not here."

"Not here?" asked Sheila, feigning stunned surprise. "Then who are *you?*"

No response.

"Are you Geraldine?"

Karen produced a happy squeal. "Yes!"

"Geraldine" was born in that moment. Her birth was totally unanticipated. Neither Sheila nor Karen had planned her arrival, and certainly Barbara and I were taken by surprise, but there was no denying her existence from that Saturday morning onward. Geraldine became Karen's alter ego. Karen gave Geraldine full credit for all noteworthy achievements, and when Karen failed at something or misbehaved, Geraldine got the blame. Geraldine was responsible for all the good crawling, all the milk spilling—and on Karen's obstinate days it was

Geraldine who balked at co-operating with our patterning teams.

Geraldine lived with us throughout the summer of 1968, and just at the point when Barbara began to express concern that this newcomer might be an unhealthy influence on Karen—an excuse for a little girl frustrated by her own incapacities to seek another identity—Geraldine apparently decided to make a new life for herself. At least I assume that was the case, because after a few months as a member of our family Geraldine began disappearing for days at a time, reappearing now and again when we least expected her, for comic relief rather than to obstruct the program.

Geraldine was fun while she lasted, and I'm delighted she was able to come. Most important, I think she gave us some clues to Karen's emerging personality. Karen was becoming a young lady with an impish sense of humor and a keen imagination, a streak of stubborn determination and a yen for independence.

Most children seem to learn independence and defiance simultaneously—but not Karen. She had her share of mulish moments, but she had struggled hard against the shackles of dependency and knew that none of the skills that gave her freedom had been won with tantrums, and none of her independence won with petulance.

Independence was joy. When I tried to hold Karen's hand so she could pass a Ry-Krisp to a hungry burro at a zoo in nearby Springfield, through a fence she could not really see, Karen pleaded, "Please don't help me, Daddy. I want to do it myself."

Karen's Lefty took a small step toward independence by learning to "make the bell ring" on my Underwood 21, as a reward for pressing the space bar a number of times—and Righty mastered the technique of lifting a drink to Karen's lips, after we discovered that a glass container designed to hold a frozen shrimp cocktail is the best of tumblers for a little girl whose stiff fingers don't always behave as they're told.

In a park one day we discovered a Karen-sized chair swing

—a swing Karen could use without having to hold on, or balance herself—and we lost no time in ordering one from a playground-equipment company. Unfortunately, the new swing provided an opportunity for sister Gretchen to exert *her* independence.

"My swing!" Gretchen insisted when the package arrived in the mail and was unwrapped. But the swing proved slightly too large for Gretch; twice when John was pushing her she slipped under the restraining bar and onto the ground, and after that decided that pushing was more fun than being pushed.

Karen was radiant as she experienced for the first time the sensation of swinging "by myself," with a summery breeze swirling her hair.

"I push Kana . . . Kana swing!" declared Gretchen.

"Two sisters on the swing," Karen responded. "Two sisters together."

We told Karen of the independent little girl who used to come to my office door to announce, "Du-why-dye!" ("Dinner ready, Daddy!") and one noontime she decided she was ready to assume that responsibility again.

Not the sound of running feet and an impatient rap on the door this time, but as much enthusiasm as ever. "Daddy!" came the cry from the bottom of the back stairs which led to my office. "Daddy dee-uh—I'm coming to get you."

I appeared on the landing at the head of the stairs and looked down at a lovely sight—Karen struggling to ascend the stairs, needing a boost but reaching ahead one stair tread at a time in a series of movements that The Institutes wouldn't have recognized but no doubt would have approved.

"Where are you going, Karen?" I asked.

Karen stopped short when she heard my voice. "Go back!" she commanded. "I'm coming to get you."

Increasing mobility certainly had a great deal of bearing on Karen's increasing sense of independence. The day our friend Ellen Riggs drove down from Winchester, Massachusetts, to have lunch, to restock our dwindling supply of her famous candied orange rind, and to inspect the condition of the chimney swifts who had taken up residence in one of our disused chimneys, Karen marked the occasion by struggling across the kitchen floor to the porch door in record time, shouting, "Get out of the way, Daddy!" and "Look out, Doc!"

Karen soon learned, with no encouragement from her parents, to push herself off her bed following her afternoon nap and to do some upstairs exploring. She spent so much time crawling on her tummy that the fronts of her clothes began wearing out before the backs ever really got dirty.

When Barbara went on sick leave for a couple of days and Flo D'Aleo and Sally Masters took charge of the program, Karen's increasing mobility caused Sally to make a confession.

"We had a hard time getting through Karen's program," Sally apologized. "All she wanted to do was crawl!"

All she wanted to do was crawl. . . . We could learn to be grateful for problems such as that.

"Wet sand is the best possible medium for crawling," an Institutes staff member had told us on our first re-evaluation visit to Stenton Avenue the previous February, and that piece of advice had fallen on receptive ears. We liked wet sand, thought a little wet sand would do us all good, and hadn't really seen any since Karen's illness. I announced that it didn't appear I was on the verge of supporting the family in grand style as a playwright or essayist, so wouldn't it be a good idea if I went back to work, perhaps in a warm place where wet sand was accessible and where little girls could crawl around in light clothing throughout the year, unencumbered by winter woolens and far from drafty floors? Barbara, a "warm-weather person," responded that I really hadn't given playwriting and essaying a fair trial, but that if I insisted on moving nearer some nice wet sand she would not stand in the way of progress.

So I clipped a couple of help-wanted ads from *Editor & Publisher* magazine and composed letters of application. One ad was for a post as journalistic adviser in Pago Pago, American

Samoa; the other was for the managership of the Bermuda News Bureau, in Hamilton, Bermuda.

We were glad to have an excuse to reread Margaret Mead's *Coming of Age in Samoa,* sitting around a candle-lit dining room with Gail and Rob Ellis, contemplating life in a South Seas society where people are suspicious of walls. Visions of palm-fringed beaches remained very much in our minds as we concentrated on the day-to-day task of moving Karen up the neurological ladder—but the chances of landing such a post seemed as remote as the posts themselves.

Meanwhile Karen had revisited The Institutes in mid-May and again in late July—we were given an appointment for re-evaluation every ten or twelve weeks—and we had been given quite a few new and innovative activities to incorporate into her program.

To force Karen to push better with her left leg, we were to put an inflatable splint on her right leg for short periods. We introduced cross-pattern crawling—left arm and right leg moving in unison, then right arm and left leg. We put strips of molding across the slide at given intervals so that Karen might learn to pull herself uphill. The huskier of our patterners administered a weight-bearing program, wrapping Karen's fingers around a section of broom-handle-sized pole, then lifting pole and Karen for a two-minute swing before patterning time. To enhance her visual appreciation of detail, we were to buy a slide projector and to make color slides of familiar, well-outlined objects. Because she tended to use only one eye at a time and seemed in danger of developing a "lazy eye," we were to begin patching her eyes alternately. And finally, we were to try Karen on a reading program, introducing her to a selection of words printed in very large red letters—"ball," "Daddy," "Mommy," "apple," "red," and the like.

We were somewhat dubious about the reading program, and a final visit to our neurologist did not allay our concern. He seemed genuinely impressed when he examined Karen, but as skeptical as before when we reported that the Institutes wanted us to try teaching Karen to read.

"If she ever has enough vision to read" was his reply. "And I seriously doubt that she will."

He had ordered another EEG and said the results showed Karen's brain waves to be "entirely within the normal limits for her age." We were told the report was "encouraging," but that Karen obviously was not fully recovered—"clinical problems remain."

We didn't understand then what these EEG tests proved—and still don't understand—but were greatly disappointed that neurology had so little to offer Karen, that neurologists and The Institutes were practically not on speaking terms. We continued to see a neurologist because we dared not stop hedging our bets, because The Institutes, after all, had no neurologist on their staff. Yet it seemed as if we were going to this specialist merely to confirm that Karen was indeed progressing under The Institutes program, and to demonstrate to him that he had been amiss in advising us that we would very likely be wasting our money by taking Karen to Philadelphia.

(Well, he admitted, speaking as a parent and not as a neurologist, in our situation he might well have done just as we did.)

We failed to teach Karen to read that summer, and the summer after that, but that fact didn't diminish the thrill of sharing her excitement as she made new discoveries with her eyes:

June 17:

I hold Karen up to the mirror in the downstairs bathroom. "I see the baby!" she cries. There is a pause, then a second discovery: "It's Karen Luise!" Yet even then she can't quite believe that she is looking at her own image, for she says, "I want to touch the baby," and Righty reaches out to touch the mirror.

August 14:

Karen is able to identify color photos of Gretchen and "the ball" when we project them on a wall. (But she still can't distinguish a photo of dark-haired Mommy from one of dark-haired patterner Irene King.)

August 25:

It's dark, well past the children's bedtime, and we are re-turning home from the St. Adalbert's Church bazaar, from merry-go-round rides and cotton candy. We're driving along Enfield Street, and as we pause for a traffic signal at the North Main Street intersection, a streetlamp from in front of the Mobil station creates a play of light and shadow in the front seat.

I give Karen's hand a squeeze, and she says, a trifle sleepily, "I see you, Daddy."

Karen has seen me before, in the daylight, but here in the darkness, I assume, she is "seeing" me once again with her fingertips. "I know, Karen," is my only response.

Karen realizes that I have failed to comprehend. "No, Daddy," she says, more urgently this time. "I see you with my eyes, not my hands."

I shiver. The back seat cheering section sends up a cry. *I see you with my eyes . . .*

August 28:

Large subjects not directly in front of Karen—the sky, the trees, the road—remain incomprehensible to her, and in an effort to expand her range of vision, we take her outside during a severe lightning storm. She seems impressed and a bit fright-ened. "Make the lights go out," she requests.

I explain that only God can do that. She ponders my reply for a moment, then shouts: "God! Put those lights out!"

September 24:

During lunch today, Karen's eyes identify a radio on the kitchen counter.

Later, in the playroom, she asks, "What's that, Mommy?"

Barbara is puzzled by the question. "What is it you're looking at, Karen?"

"The red ball," Karen replies.

Her "What's that?" appears to have been not so much a direct question as a desire that her hunch be confirmed.

September 30:

Karen reads her first book. There are no words in the book—just large color photos of simple objects against a plain background. An egg on one page, an orange on the next, a set of keys on the next. Our Colorado friends, Rosemary and Ted Tedesco, had presented the book during a visit in July, and Karen has succeeded in committing most of the objects to memory. She's not yet capable of recognizing keys or a cup in another picture situation, but she knows *these* keys and *this* cup, and that is progress.

October 8:

The retired news editor of the *Press* had mounted a set of five large white letters—K, A, R, E, and N—on vividly colored squares of plastic, and after a couple months of exposure to them, Karen has managed to identify the correct letter and color for four out of five. The feat was achieved yesterday, and today one of our patterning ladies attempts to induce a demonstration. The five letters are laid out in front of our daughter in sequence—*KAREN*.

"Now . . . what's your name, dear?" Karen is asked.

"Geraldine" is her immediate reply.

One Indian summer afternoon, Geraldine, Barbara, Sheila, Mary Jo, and I were taking a tea break on the back porch. Someone mentioned Dr. Crowley. We wondered if he had completed his year's study at the University of Minnesota and decided we should phone someday soon to find out and perhaps invite him to dinner.

The conditions for telepathic communication must have been excellent that day, for within an hour Joe Crowley, entirely unannounced, was parking his car in our driveway.

"Unbelievable," he declared after a few minutes with Karen, "that she has done this in one year."

We talked about the elapsed year, and when patterning time came around again, we invited our otolaryngological friend to witness some of Karen's prescribed activities, and in fact to "do the head."

"Want Dr. Crowley to do it again," Karen declared when the bell on the timer rang—a signal honor, for Karen had never before requested an extension of a patterning-table session.

Two days later we received another important call—this time from the mid-Atlantic. A Bermuda Government official was phoning to advise me that I had been approved for the manager-ship of the Bermuda News Bureau and that we were invited to move family and furnishings to Bermuda aboard the Cunard Line's S.S. *Franconia* as soon as I could settle our affairs in Connecticut.

We rejoiced—and swallowed hard. Selling our home and our Tiny House, making decisions over which of our posses-sions should be sold (refrigerator, dress-making dummy, leaf incinerator), which stored in the Ellises' attic (heavy coats, half our books), which given away (sofa bed, sleds, Karen's slide), which taken with us—doing all that while keeping Karen's program going and finding some time for my writing would be difficult enough, but how were we going to find the words to say good-by to all the people who had given so magnificently of themselves in Karen's behalf?

We had prepared John, by means of an unscrupulous strata-gem, for the eventuality of leaving his Enfield friends. Some-how—I can't recall how—we had convinced him that the notion of moving to a land of surf and sand was *his* idea, and by the time we had confirmation of the Bermuda assignment John had already suggested that we should move to "an ocean house" one of these days.

John was at his kindergarten when the Bermuda call came through, so the girls were the first to be confronted with the news of our impending move. Neither had any idea what the word "Bermuda" meant, so we simply asked the two of them how they would like to live in "an ocean house."

Karen kicked her legs and beamed. "Yes, Daddy!" she said with unrestrained enthusiasm.

Gretchen shook her head vigorously and said, "No," period. She declined to elaborate.

That afternoon I went out to do some shopping and stopped at Cutter Lane to break the news to Sheila and Mary Jo, who were across-the-street neighbors.

"Go ahead," said Sheila. "Move to Bermuda. See if we care. . . . Just don't take Karen."

"So far away?" asked Mary Jo.

Mary Jo didn't make it easy to follow through on our decision—and neither did patterner Brenda Tartaglione.

"Gee," said Brenda. "Do you have to? Working with Karen seems like the most worthwhile thing I've ever done."

"I'll surely miss John's visits," declared Emma Stewart, our ninety-one-year-old neighbor. "And I'll miss your bringing me my mail from the post office every morning, too. But Bermuda will be good for Karen, won't it?"

"Yes," I replied, hoping it would.

Our pediatrician said he thought the move would be a good one, that he looked forward to hearing of Karen's progress via reports from The Institutes—and that he felt Bermuda had erred in permitting both cars *and* motorbikes, when the colony's bar against motor vehicles was dropped in 1946.

John lost his first tooth—accidentally punched out by Matthew Descy—a couple of weeks before we left Enfield.

I began cultivating a moustache so that I would look correct in British Bermuda, and one of our young friends allowed as how this new hirsute adornment made me appear "very extinguished."

We had a farewell round of handshakes and good-lucks at the *Press,* and I attended my final meetings at Enfield organizations I had served—Big Brothers, the mental health clinic, the teen center, the redevelopment authority. Hardest of all was standing up during the eleven o'clock service at First Presbyterian and uttering a few extemporaneous, emotional, inadequate, heartfelt words of thanks to those who had had a hand in Karen's recovery.

Barbara held a gala farewell buffet lunch for the battalion of patterners Karen knew collectively as "my ladies." Karen's program was carried on right up to the bittersweet end, and her patterning table was the last object to be carried to the van.

Nana and Grandpop's red brick house just outside Philadelphia served as our last home in the United States for the few days while our household goods were being crated for shipment and delivered to Pier 92 in New York.

Our friends the Streibigs, the tactile-board makers, who lived only fifteen minutes from Barbara's parents, livened those last days by holding a joint party for our five children, to celebrate the five birthdays of the previous year, the impending arrival of Streibig Child No. 3, and Karen's progress. A year earlier we had held a similar Breisky-Streibig party in Enfield, and Karen had been so terrified by the noisemakers and mechanical toys that Barbara had had to take her away from the table to stop her screaming and to calm her. But now, on the eve of our departure for her new life in Bermuda, Karen was a different child—a trim and inquisitive tummy-crawler, visually bewildered but boundlessly affectionate, helpless but cheerful, a gregarious gamine with a wandering eye and a wondering mind. She joined happily in the noisemaking, giving us all the more reason to celebrate.

While we were loading our rented station wagon for the trip to New York and the *Franconia,* Nana inspired Karen toward presenting us all a farewell gift: Karen got up on her knees by herself, for the first time.

So it was that on a cloudy, drizzly November 9, Nana Liz came down from Westchester to Pier 92, and Nana and Grandpop followed us from Philadelphia on the New Jersey Turnpike. A New York chum named Mahoney brought farewell chocolates for the children, and I arranged champagne for the grown-ups.

Our ship's horn blew. There were hugs all around, departures down the gangplank, and we unfurled streamers over the railing as tugs pushed us away from *Franconia*'s berth, nudging us on our way to a new life under a warm sun.

CHAPTER IX

Bermuda

The Bermuda Islands—reef-fringed, fishhook-shaped, balmy and beautiful—were discovered by Juan de Bermúdez of Spain in 1503 and by the Breiskys of Connecticut in November of 1968, on Remembrance Day.

Several weeks earlier I had flown down as an advance party of one, on a reconnoitering mission to find a suitable roof to put over our heads, to check the price of ground chuck, and to assure myself that we would be happy on this twenty-two-square-mile pinprick of land some six hundred miles off the coast of North Carolina. The mission had been a reasonably successful one: I had found a white, limestone-block, semi-furnished home called Whistling Winds, perched near the top of Cottage Hill in Hamilton Parish. The house was a bit remote, the rent was a trifle high for our budget, and we would be obliged to pay an additional sum to put the owner's furniture in storage—but we could look out over the sun-dappled waters of Harrington Sound, and hibiscus and poinsettia would be blooming for Christmas.

What's more, I had lined up some prospective patterning ladies. In the Rentals Unlimited office (where available rentals proved very limited indeed), I had met the pastor of the Peace Lutheran Church. By that time I was not at all shy about recruiting help for Karen. I told this young clergyman in the red Bermuda shorts that my wife was a Lutheran and that we were hoping to find a church home with a ladies' guild which might offer us a hand—in fact, several pairs of hands. He said he was certain he could be of some help.

In the produce department of a Hamilton supermarket where I was checking prices for Barbara, I asked a fellow customer if the large green object I was inspecting was a papaw. The object proved to be a Bermuda avocado and the customer proved, in a few weeks' time, to be an excellent patterning lady.

Steaming out of New York Harbor and into Hamilton Harbour with three small children, one jittery schnauzer, and a houseful of furniture was high adventure for all concerned, but the hours of torment between departure and arrival—pitching and rolling across angry seas which seemed oblivious to us, as if we had wandered by accident into a battle among giant waves—are recalled only hazily. Even the nurse assigned to duty in the children's playroom of S.S. *Franconia* was laid low by mal de mer. Our solicitous cabin steward prescribed Coke, saltines, apples, and seasickness pills, and when we were ready to try something more substantial, he repaired to some private galley and rustled up scrambled eggs, which baby Gretchen carried, spoonful by spoonful, to the four members of her family who remained horizontal in our two adjoining staterooms.

Samuel Clemens once wrote that Bermuda is heaven on earth, but that you have to go through hell to get there. Mr. Clemens must have booked passage at the tail end of the cruiseship season, as we had. We shared his enthusiasm about this heaven on earth, certainly, but would have settled for something less after that painful but mercifully short voyage. Due to a lashing rainstorm, we hadn't been able to go abovedeck even once during the trip, so the bright sun, the gleaming white rooftops, the Old World pastel-colored shops of Front Street—and the firm ground—seemed especially appealing as we stepped ashore.

Because we arrived on a holiday, our seven cases of furnishings and assorted other belongings could not be off-loaded until the following day; so it had been arranged that we would spend our first night in Bermuda at Deepdene Manor, a small hotel across Harrington Sound from Whistling Winds.

We were met at dockside by a pair of onions (the highest praise one may bestow upon a Bermudian), my model secretary-to-be, Vicky Hamshere, and the Department of Tourism's executive secretary. After giving Doc a good sniff of Front Street, we made our way to Deepdene Manor, where we shared a patio lunch with the cheekiest gang of sparrows I have ever seen, then changed into swimsuits for a sample of swimming-in-November, in a pool set among citrus trees and hibiscus, and morning glories that flourished in the afternoon.

We had a wing to ourselves at Deepdene—two large rooms off a corridor behind the main desk. Barbara, Karen and Gretchen occupied one room, and the boys—John, Dad and Doc—occupied the other. Crawling from the girls' room to the boys' on her tummy, Karen attracted the attention of the lovely wife of Deepdene's manager. We signed her on the spot as a patterner.

We could hear Doc's yowling all the way from the dining room that evening and imagined the management and guests of Deepdene Manor were not disappointed to learn that we would be checking out after breakfast the following day.

Strong southwesterly winds were whipping around Whistling Winds when the moving men commenced uncrating our belongings outside the kitchen door. Our lawn soon looked blizzard-struck as countless bits of shredded packing paper were picked up by the wind, deposited in shrubs and hedges, and hung on tufts of grass. A posse of neighborhood children was formed spontaneously to organize a cleanup detail, and John soon discovered that his new home was surrounded by an abundance of boys ("buys," they called themselves) his age.

Having no urgent office duties to perform, my new secretary, Vicky, volunteered to serve as grocery shopper and dish-unpacker that day. She spread peanut-butter-and-strawberry-jam sandwiches with the only utensil we could find—a yellow plastic swizzle stick—and when we had fitted the patterning-table top over a kitchen counter, we initiated her into the mysteries of "doing the head."

Early impressions and images of Whistling Winds and of life in Bermuda:

. . . Barbara's discovery, through our bedroom window one morning (before she had located her glasses), of a bush covered with blue flowers. Suddenly the "flowers" took flight. They were bluebirds.

. . . No billboards, no neon signs.

. . . John as pillion passenger on a rented Dutch motorbike, clinging to my waist as we explored Fractious Street and points south.

. . . A weekly power failure. Karen petrified—frightened beyond reason—when the lights went out during our evening meal. What fears raced through her mind in those first seconds? She wouldn't, or couldn't, say.

. . . Neighbors closing their shutters at dusk.

. . . Embarrassment resulting from the Bermudian system of interviewing "head teachers" and selecting your child's school, rather than simply going where you're told. Perhaps 90 per cent of the kids in the nearest school, Francis Patton, were black, and I hoped their black, bright and captivating head teacher wouldn't think I was probing the quality of education at her school for that reason. ("Well," she said, "my son went here and he's a scholarship student at Yale right now." So we decided Francis Patton would be just fine for John.)

. . . Barbara trying to cope with a bawling two-year-old Bermudian visitor: "What do you want, dear?" "Bicket!" "*Bicket?* Wouldn't you like a cookie?" "Bicket!" ("Bicket," we discovered, is two-year-old Bermudian talk for "biscuit," which is English for "cookie.")

. . . Toads. Tiny ones, half the size of your thumb, whistling in harmony in the trees at night. Mammoth ones, lugubrious mini-monsters, making a home in our basement-level laundry room. (Barbara, firmly: "Sorry, but I'm not going down there at night. If you want your blue socks out of the dryer, you'll have to go down and get them for yourself.")

. . . The total stillness of late evening being broken as a

neighbor made his way home strumming his guitar and singing, "What a friend we have in Jesus."

. . . And Karen, not only standing on her knees with relative ease but assuming the role of solicitous big sister by mimicking her mother: "Now tell us what you want, Gretchen. We can't help you unless you tell us what's the matter."

Keeping to the left-hand side of British Bermuda's winding roads seemed easy enough, but Hamilton's street pattern threw me and I failed my automobile driver's test at first try, which meant three more weeks of grocery shopping by motorbike. Karen, meanwhile, was moving ahead on all four cylinders: Not long after our arrival in Bermuda, she got up off her tummy and onto her hands and knees. She was ready to graduate from "crawling" to "creeping."

Progression to creeping is a very significant step for any toddler who is achieving mobility. Most children decide for themselves when they're ready to commence getting around on hands and knees, but Karen needed priming. The Institutes had prescribed a rubber mat to provide a slipproof surface she could push against. Barbara and I prescribed *The Little Engine That Could*, a children's classic which both John and Karen had demanded repeatedly at bedtime.

The heroine of *The Little Engine That Could* is the Little Blue Engine, who declares, "They use me only for switching trains in the yard—I have never been over the mountain," when the trainload of dolls and toys beg her to pull them to "the good little boys and girls on the other side of the mountain." At length the little engine is prevailed upon to do her best. She hitches herself to the trainload of toys, and puffs and puffs and chugs and chugs, saying, "I think I can—I think I can—I think I can—" until at last the summit has been scaled.

So Karen on her rubber mat became the Little Blue Engine scaling the mountain. And Barbara or I, kneeling behind her, our hands supporting her while she tried balancing and moving ahead on hands and knees, became the trainload of toys.

"Let's go, Little Blue Engine!"

"I think I can." Puff. Chug. "I think I can."

And before we knew it Karen was creeping forward, and reciting with pride the chant of the Little Blue Engine as she puffed happily down the far side of the mountain—

"I thought I could.

I thought I could.

I thought I could."

On an island that enjoys overemployment, where working wives are the rule rather than the exception, and where time schedules are not always taken seriously, once-a-week "patterning ladies" proved difficult to find in quantity. We did, however, soon develop a strong nucleus.

The Miller sisters—Connie, Judy, Patty—of Peace Lutheran Church, took charge of Saturday mornings.

Peace ladies Ethel, June, Henrietta, Luella, Dorothy, Kim and Peggy joined the roster, as did the pastor himself.

The wife of the news bureau's director of photography became a regular.

A Brownie leader came—and brought visual aids made by her daughter's troop.

A Peace Lutheran lady named Eileen Outerbridge recruited her husband's cousin-in-law, Rosemary, to go along with her, and she spoke about Karen before the Rotary Club's Inner Wheel group.

Hilda Aitkin heard Eileen speak, volunteered herself and her husband, Robin. (The Aitkins, both in their seventies, became virtually substitute grandparents to our girls; their presence—and the sack of Bermuda citrus they often brought from their orchard—invariably buoyed Karen.)

Hilda Aitkin also recruited two women from *her* church— Edith and Edna.

Edna brought a bridge-playing friend, Eleanor.

Eleanor brought sunshine and laughter—and soon we were in business.

The mainstay of the program, however, was our next-door neighbor, Arian Francis, who not only volunteered to come several times a week but asked to be called "any time you need me." Barbara could no longer summon me with a rap on a steam pipe when a patterning lady failed to appear—but she could summon Arian. And she had Arian's "aunt-in-law"—"Aunt Helen" to the entire neighborhood, seventy-five years of steadfast faith and boundless good cheer. Life in Whistling Winds, Cottage Hill, Bailey's Bay, Bermuda, would not have been half so pleasant for Barbara and the girls without Arian and Aunt Helen close at hand.

I tend, for no logical reason, to measure Karen's progress each Christmastime—to reflect, over that holiday period, how Karen has advanced since the previous Christmas. On our first Christmas in Bermuda, we recalled that Karen could not crawl on her tummy a year previous and that now, at the age of three years, eight months, she was able to take half a dozen steps on her hands and knees before collapsing. Her fingers were becoming more skilled at distinguishing a thruppence from a shilling, but she still had difficulty telling a shilling from half a crown. Perhaps most significant—one Christmas ago she was barely conscious of the lights on the tree, and colors meant nothing to her; this year she tried to help decorate the tree and could fish through a pile of cards in search of "Santa in his red suit."

We knew we were in Bermuda when we discovered a blue-tailed lizard climbing onto the angel after we had trimmed our pint-sized Canadian evergreen. When the butcher told me our Christmas turkey would come to twelve pounds, I had to ask, "Is that the weight or the price?" Barbara served the obligatory side dish of cassava pie (pork, chicken, cassava root) with our turkey, and we built a yule fire of Bermuda cedar. And on Boxing Day (December 26) the Francises—Arian, Arliss, Antony and Antonette—trooped over from next door with a pitcher of rum swizzle.

Nana and Grandpop flew down from Philadelphia for the

holidays—the impetus behind Karen's creeping effort had been largely to "show Nana," Karen declared—and Grandpop declined to remove the Scottish tam-o'-shanter we gave him except at mealtime and bedtime. A pair of beautiful Italian-made dolls were the grandparents' gifts to our girls, leading Karen to insist that her beloved new "baby" be put on a regular patterning schedule. John, aged five, was presented an English two-wheeler, and John and I made a snowball or two with frost scraped from the weary, overworked freezer compartment of our rented refrigerator. (Selling our Enfield fridge had been a large mistake.)

The Kirchmeiers phoned from Enfield, U.S.A., to wish us a merry Christmas. Wilfred Keller, whom an eighteen-month-old Karen had adored when he was painting our Enfield Street home, sent Karen a five-dollar check and a prayer. And Karen, out of the blue, said to anyone who cared to listen, "Mary Jo —please come to Bermuda to see me."

I came home from work on New Year's Eve on my new blue Honda cycle, and Karen greeted me with, "Daddy, what did you bring me?"

I tried to look terribly disappointed at this self-centered form of greeting, but Karen was not yet very good at reading expressions.

"Is that," I asked, "the right way to say hello to Daddy?"

"Daddy, *please*, what did you bring me?" was Karen's response.

On New Year's Day we were invited to join a party of Bermudians for a picnic at Horseshoe Beach. We wore sweaters, and the wind blew sand on our deviled eggs, and 1969 was under way.

January 1969: It's fine to stand in the doorway to Karen's room and see her up on her knees, chatting with her "baby." . . . And it is fine to be able to record more small discoveries— the discovery by Righty of a nostril ("Hey, Daddy, there's a hole in my face") and of a door handle in our car ("What's this?" Karen asks, and suddenly the door is ajar).

Returning to Bermuda from The Institutes in early February, Karen was especially proud to anounce that "I had an airplane lunch." (She had been unable to see the airplane she boarded —it was simply too large to comprehend—but she had no trouble seeing every item on her lunch tray.) Her increased mobility moved her a notch past a neurological age of twenty-four months on The Institutes' developmental profile, and Barbara was told to emphasize improvement in creeping.

Creeping is the key, said the IAHP, because mobility and seeing are interlocking brain functions, and creeping introduces an infant to a three-dimensional visual world. We were advised to abandon the reading program for the time being, but to introduce some eye-convergence exercises and to try some new methods of making Karen use her eyes and hands together— "building" with blocks, pouring, lying on her back and catching a balloon, unscrewing the cap from a plastic bottle, banging objects together.

Karen was given a special reward at the end of that visit to The Institutes: For crossing a room on her hands and knees for the first time, she was granted permission to tug on the beard of Institutes director Glenn Doman.

A few weeks later it was my turn to be given a special creeping demonstration. I had been sentenced to an indefinite term in the isolation ward of King Edward VII Memorial Hospital, with a splendid case of hepatitis, and the children joined Barbara on four of her trips to the hospital. Barbara would come up to my room and don a mask, while Nana Liz, who had flown down to help with the children, oversaw Karen's creeping demonstrations in the grassy courtyard beneath my window.

A bout with acute icteric hepatitis was not what we had in mind when we decided on a move to Bermuda. All of us suffered a bit during the five weeks I spent on my back.

For me, the pain was in the form of nausea, malaise, and bad jokes about liver ailments. ("How's your liver? Wurst?")

For Barbara, the trauma was emotional rather than physical. Watching Gretchen bound ahead of Karen in skills requiring hands, legs, and eyes in good working order. Suffering thoughtless stares in the supermarket. Feeling rage and sorrow as a boozed-up truck driver shouted from the cab of his truck while Barbara was pushing Karen in a stroller, "Hey, lady—that little girl's big enough to walk!" Puzzling over Karen's vision: How is it that she is unable to see Arian Francis standing outside the house next door, or her new pair of sunglasses held within an arm's length of her face, yet is able to announce, "There's a fly on your dish"?

We had learned to live with such hurts and frustrations, but they were more difficult for Barbara to endure when I was in the hospital and she had to cope with them alone. Barbara and I have our share of differences, but have made the obvious discovery that differences can be constructive and useful more often than they are nettlesome and eroding. In working with Karen, Barbara has usually been the one to restrain the helping hand and to insist that Karen do things for herself, while I've been too quick to say, "Let Daddy do it." Conversely, Barbara has had to call on me from time to time for a shot of optimism. I have insisted all along—faith bolstered with logic and past performance—that Karen was going to make it, and there have been times when Barbara has needed this assurance.

I, in turn, owe my optimism to Karen.

I suppose parental concern, and the concern of her patterning teams, has rubbed off on Karen, helped shape her positive outlook on life. But we deserve only a small part of the credit. Karen has inspired us far more often than we have inspired her. Somehow, she has managed to offset each slow period with some new achievement at just the right moment and to balance or overcome each moment of despondency with a moment of laughter or an hour of joy.

So it was that Karen checkmated the supermarket stares

Karen as a healthy, happy baby, in 1965 with brother John.

Home from the hospital in 1967, after the terrible assault on her brain. Karen was blind, helpless, speechless—and miserable.

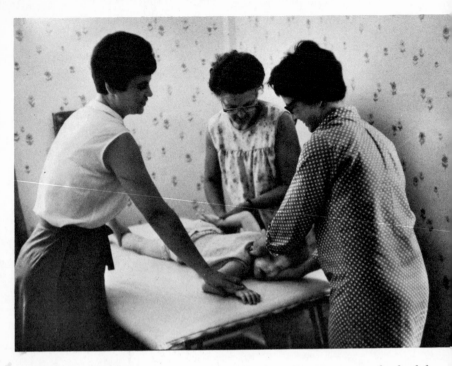

A team of patterning ladies—"one to do the right side, one to do the left and one to do the head."

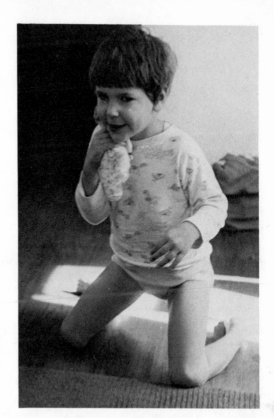

Right: "She must learn to crawl before she can creep, and to knee-walk before she can walk." *Below:* Karen, aged five, takes a few hesitant steps from her Nana Liz to her mother.

Karen (with neighbor Adela) at work with her overhead ladder—a coordination exercise inspired by tree-swinging apes.

Below: Reading lesson with Adela.

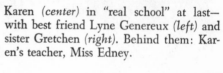

Karen *(center)* in "real school" at last—with best friend Lyne Genereux *(left)* and sister Gretchen *(right)*. Behind them: Karen's teacher, Miss Edney.

Suspended by the ankles—an improbable therapy for vision—Karen attracts Gretchen's curiosity.

Karen with one of those most responsible for her recovery—Glenn Doman,
director of the Institutes for the Achievement of Human Potential—on stage
at the 1972 convention of the United Steelworkers of America. Karen made
a little speech to the steelworkers, who help support the Institutes.

The program continues. *Left:* Karen wears special glasses to help her use her eyes together. *(Photo by Vince Cavaleri).* *Below:* Karen in traction to improve her balance.

The Breiskys, at home in Bermuda. Helping Karen "make it" has nourished the life of the whole family. *(Photo by Gene Ray)*.

(which, because of her limited vision, she was not aware of) with a joke on that same day. (Barbara, to Nana Liz after dinner: "Could you stand some coffee?" Karen, before Nana Liz had a chance to respond: "I could stand some chocolate ice cream!")

And she managed to trump her own momentary defeatism with a new and major achievement. John and Gretchen were scampering around the house one evening shortly after I returned from the hospital, and Karen was trying to keep up. After a while she quit the chase, slumped, sighed, and said simply, "Daddy?"—meaning, "Please come play with me so I won't have to compete with those two." Yet just one day later she pulled herself onto her feet for the first time.

This upstanding event took place shortly after story hour. The children were in their pajamas, and we had just read a little book received from the Streibigs of Philadelphia—*Love Is a Special Way of Feeling*. We spoke for a while of the concept of love; then I reached for Karen's hands and said simply, "Stand up."

After pulling herself onto her knees, she raised one knee at a time until her feet were flat on the floor and she was squatting; then, wobbly and determined as a young colt, she pulled herself upright while my hands balanced her.

No warm-up exercises. No fuss or fanfare. She simply stood up. Typical Karen. A round of cheers followed, of course, and she insisted on repeating the procedure until *we* were tired.

Standing with helping hands—that was Karen's present to us for her own fourth birthday, and for Easter 1969. John and Barbara built traditional Bermuda three-stick kites for Good Friday, and we followed our Bermudian neighbors' example by feasting on hot cross buns and fish cakes. The island's Easter lily crop was wrecked by salt spray that spring, but Karen was learning to sing as well as stand, so we decided it was a very nice springtime indeed. When Nana Liz had arrived in Bermuda, Karen got around by creeping on hands and knees only 25 per cent of the time, crawled on her tummy the rest of the time. Seven weeks later, as Nana Liz was preparing to return to New York, Karen resorted to tummy-crawling only when she was very tired or when an obstacle such as a slippery throw rug got in her way.

The day for Nana Liz's departure came, and Karen promised, "When you come back, I'm gonna walk for you."

Needless to say, we wished Nana Liz many happy returns to Bermuda, beginning as soon as possible.

CHAPTER X

Kathleen (alias Käthe)

The three greatest influences on four-year-old Karen in the summer of 1969 were the ocean, an overhead ladder, and Kathleen Kirchmeier—and not necessarily in that order.

But let's take them in that order.

The Ocean

We were picnicking at John Smith's Bay one Sunday in midspring, weeks before Bermudians give any serious thought to their beaches. The wind was up—a brisk wind—so we were sitting well back from the water when Karen made her announcement:

"I see the blue ocean."

How often we had stood on some promontory overlooking the sea and said, "See the ocean, Karen?" and received for a reply a simple no or pursed lips and a bowed head turning slowly from side to side, as if she were ashamed that she couldn't see that vast ocean which everyone else saw so effortlessly.

But during our Sunday picnic at John Smith's Bay, she suddenly announced that she was now able to comprehend the blue Atlantic, and furthermore that she was intrigued by the wind-whipped surf which came crashing over the sandy beach:

"I see the blue ocean. . . . There's some white stuff in it!"

The Overhead Ladder

Australopithecus, the so-called missing link between anthropoid ape and man, was identified nearly half a century ago at the University of the Witwatersrand in Johannesburg, South Africa, by a young anatomy professor–anthropologist named Dr. Raymond A. Dart.

In the mid-1960s IAHP directors Glenn Doman and Carl Delacato became convinced that there exists a missing link between creeping and walking—an explanation of how man's forebears learned to stand erect after millennia of getting around on all fours.

Doman and Delacato met Dart in South Africa, and late in 1966 Dr. Dart became the first occupant of the United Steelworkers Chair of Anthropology at the Avery Postgraduate Institutes of the Institutes for the Achievement of Human Potential. There, Doman, Delacato and Dart theorized that if swinging from limb to limb was an evolutionary stage in the emergence of man, and straightened his body into an erect position, enabling him to walk, then a substitute for low-hanging tree limbs might help brain-injured children to walk.

On May 14, 1969, Glenn Doman told Barbara, "We want you to build an overhead ladder for Karen. We think it will help her progress to knee-walking, and from knee-walking to walking on her feet."

Karen's "missing link" was to be built of half a dozen lengths of lumber, about a dozen and a half pieces of ¾-inch dowel to serve as rungs, four lengths of 1¼-inch galvanized pipe (threaded one end), four floor flanges, and four pipe clamps. The result would be a ladder with round rungs, suspended parallel to the ground at adjustable heights.

Eighteen times a day, for a minute each time, Karen was to have a go at knee-walking on her rubber creeping pad, under her overhead ladder. In due time, hopefully, we might raise the ladder so that she could walk on her feet. Not only should the ladder hasten Karen's ability to walk, Barbara was told; it should also help develop her upper body, increase her lung capacity and chest size, open up her left hand, and improve her hand-eye co-ordination.

Hardly anyone, or anything, surpasses a tree-swinging ape, Doman-Delacato-Dart claim, when it comes to lung capacity and hand-eye co-ordination.

We could reduce Karen's patterning sessions to four a day, but we should begin swinging her by her ankles, and we were to wrap her fingers around a piece of dowel and let her try to swing from that—also eighteen times a day.

Ladder work was a brand-new field at The Institutes, and the device blueprinted for us was a rather early and flimsy prototype. The overhead ladder on our porch at Whistling Winds appeared to be a missing link between a Rube Goldberg clothes-drying rack and Tarzan's playpen—but it did the job, and it was the talk of the neighborhood children.

Karen began knee-walking as soon as the ladder was installed. At first she would collapse after advancing only two or three rungs, but before long she could knee-walk the length of the ladder. Antony and Antonette Francis, Bobby Hayward, "Kong Kong," and other Cottage Hill characters would join us in applauding Karen's performance, and Karen basked in the applause—provided it was deserved. If the applause seemed premature, she would insist, "Don't clap now!" Only when she had completed a self-imposed quota of rungs would she say, "Now clap."

Kathleen

Kathleen Kirchmeier is the fifth of seven children born to our good friends Lou and Otto Kirchmeier. ("We *planned* six of them," Lou insisted when she was named chairman of Enfield's Planned Parenthood group.) Kathleen is a quick-witted and concerned citizen. She wears her hair long, her clothes loose, and has a way of appearing strong and vulnerable at the same time.

Born "Kathleen," she became "Kathy" as a youngster and was insisting on "Käthe" (usually pronounced "Kathy") when we got to know her.

It was Käthe who helped Barbara see to it that Karen attended to plenty of monkey business on the overhead ladder during our first Bermuda summer, without sacrificing her daily romp on the wet sand we had come so far to be near.

Käthe flew in at noon on Sunday, June 22, after completing her third year at Enfield High and after accepting the terms of the nonunion contract we offered her—room and board, a round-trip ticket from Hartford, and £5 (then $12.15) pocket money per week, in exchange for irregular hours and a six- or seven-day-a-week regimen of household chores, program work, baby-sitting, Gretchen-chasing, and swimming instruction. As a fringe benefit I bought a very secondhand Honda motorbike for her use.

Käthe was more useful to us in 1969 as a result of her summer of '67 experience, when she had helped a bit with the program but was expected primarily to keep baby Gretchen diapered, happy, and out of serious trouble.

Käthe came to us in the summer of 1969 with a 33-rpm reward in her suitcase—a recording of "The Little Engine That Could" for Karen ("I Think I Can") Breisky—as well as gifts for John and Gretchen. Within an hour of her arrival she had invented a piling-on-of-hands game which involved both Lefty and Righty and had begun working with Karen on her overhead ladder.

Barbara and Käthe never quite completed eighteen ladder sessions a day, however, as The Institutes had directed, because Karen thrived on achievement—on being able to manage more consecutive rungs during a single session—because eighteen sessions a day would have made the ladder monotonous rather than fun, and because we wouldn't have been able to make time every day for an afternoon session at nearby Shelly Bay beach. The beach was important to us that summer.

Shelly Bay was nearer, and safer for the children, but once a week we would go to John Smith's Bay, on the surf-splashed south shore, where the scenery is more spectacular and where the blue water has more white stuff in it.

Karen's legs churned beautifully at Shelly Bay. The buoyancy of the salt water almost made it possible for her to walk when she was waist-high, but she distrusted the rocky or grassy bottom and would ask to be picked up or to be taken to deeper water where her legs would clear the bottom and she could cling to the Yogi Bear float we had bought her—"my Yogi," she called it. Quite often the sea at Shelly Bay was flat calm, and on those occasions she would lie across our outstretched arms so that she could have the sensation of floating on her back. But it was difficult at first to get her to use her arms for anything but clinging and to show any enthusiasm for getting her face wet.

I happened to be in charge of the Saturday swimming session—the day before Käthe's arrival—when Karen immersed herself for the first time. She had had enough of the water for a while and asked to be taken back to the beach, where she could creep and "dig." While kneeling in a mound of drying sargasso weed, on the water's edge, she suddenly lost her balance and toppled forward into the drink.

I ran to her, and when I got there her arms and legs were thrashing (I have never seen Lefty work harder) and her head was completely submerged. She came up spluttering and gasping, too frightened and bewildered to think about crying. But she caught her breath soon, and by the time we got home she was boasting to anyone who would listen about "my diving."

As the worst adult swimmer in the family (devil-may-care snorkeler, you understand, but poor swimmer) I was happy to be credited with giving the first diving lesson and to leave the swimming instruction to Barbara and Käthe—mostly Käthe, because Barbara ordinarily did her shopping and errand-running during the hour that Käthe and the kids spent at Shelly Bay.

John developed enormous confidence in the water during that first of our oceanside summers, but no one really learned to swim. The sand and the sea were fine for Karen, however, and we considered it an achievement that Käthe gave her the confidence to sit waist-high in the water, keep her balance, and close her mouth and hold her nose simultaneously when a gentle wave approached. (Even though "holding my nose" usually meant merely holding onto the nose, not closing the nostrils. Karen couldn't apply enough pressure with thumb and forefinger to squeeze her nostrils shut.)

"Put some pepper in this water," Karen demanded one day after a Shelly Bay swimming lesson.

"Why, Karen?"

"Because there's too much salt in it."

There were, of course, other Käthe-induced achievements that summer.

Karen's overhead-ladder record on the day of Käthe's arrival was nine rungs. On July 6 she "did forty"; August 10, one hundred. (Bribery, it must be admitted, played a part in this improvement. Käthe headed for the neighborhood variety store every payday to find a small "surprise" which could be tied in a bag and hung from Karen's ladder. Payday for Käthe became Surprise Day for Karen.)

Käthe taught Karen to climb into bed. Karen would have to be boosted into a standing position alongside her bed, but with Käthe's help she learned to lift a leg over the edge of the bed and to scramble up.

On the day the Caribbean Black Power Conference opened in Bermuda, John announced that he would like to have an Afro cut, and Karen learned to adjust the volume on our transistor radio. (A noteworthy achievement. She still couldn't induce Righty's stubborn fingers to turn the radio off and on, but she could turn it up a little or down a little, and having achieved this skill, she became very particular about whether the radio was making "too much noise" or not enough.)

"The Eagle has landed," we learned from our radio on July 20, and Käthe gave Karen a proper lecture on the meaning of man's voyage to the moon. Karen took it all in.

On the day of the moon landing we launched our new twelve-foot inflatable dinghy in Harrington Sound, mounted our British Seagull outboard, and let Karen experience "steering." Käthe's brand-new Enfield High class ring fell to the bottom of Harrington Sound that day, and Käthe wept.

It was Käthe who sang the girls to sleep most evenings, did battle with Gretchen over Gretchen's habit of running to Mrs. Francis's house for a cookie and refusing to return, kept a record of whether it was Karen's or Gretchen's turn to "be the mommy" each time they would play house, and completely cured Karen (if not Gretchen) of fussing when left with a sitter. ("Crying," Karen informed me somewhat dubiously one summer evening, "that's baby stuff, isn't it?")

By this time Käthe was learning a great lesson from Karen: patience.

Käthe wrote me a letter from college recently in which she referred to the 1969 Käthe as "snippy." She had a low frustration point at that stage of her life, she said; patience was not her strong suit. Karen, on the other hand, not only was enormously patient herself in most situations but also demanded patience from others, not because of anything she said, but because she became, as Käthe observed, "just plain confused" when working with an impatient instructor.

In time Käthe and Karen were discussing their mutual problem openly. Käthe explained that she had always been an impatient person and that it was difficult for her to keep from doing things *for* Karen, rather than waiting for Karen to accomplish the task—and that although such an accommodation made life easier for all concerned, Käthe really wasn't doing her job and Karen really couldn't expect to make much progress that way.

"I told her," Käthe recalled in her recent letter, "that we

would both have to remember to try harder so that Karen could learn things. She *really* understood, and we agreed that practice was the best way to learn."

Käthe became so enamored of this theory of education, in fact, that she decided to experiment with it on Gretchen early one afternoon when Barbara was unloading the groceries from our car.

Three flights of outdoor stairs had to be negotiated at Whistling Winds in order to progress from the car, on the lower lawn, to the front door; so toting the groceries from car to kitchen became a major project. Before Käthe's arrival in Bermuda, each trip to the Piggly Wiggly had meant carrying Karen down and up the steps while holding Gretchen's hand, and returning two or three times for the bags of groceries. After Käthe's arrival Barbara had only half as much carrying to do, and Gretchen became a helper rather than a burden.

Käthe didn't tell Barbara that she was testing her practice-makes-perfect theory on two-and-a-half-year-old Gretchen; she simply handed Gretch a small bag and sent her on her way.

"What did you give her to carry, Käthe?" Barbara wondered.

"The eggs," Käthe replied.

"The eggs?!"

"How else is she going to learn self-confidence?"

And at that moment Gretchen created an unconfident-looking arrangement of scrambled eggs on the next-to-last step of the top flight.

Our children enjoyed two vacation treats that summer. The first was with my brother Arthur's family, in Bermuda; the second was with old friends, back in Enfield.

Inasmuch as I had bought one new and one used Honda from him in only eight months, our friendly Honda dealer must have felt that moving his wife and children in with his parents in St. George's and renting his Shelly Bay house to my brother for twelve days was the least he could do in the interest of improved customer relations. At any rate, a deal was struck, and we had Uncle Arthur, Aunt Marlene, and cousins Doug, Debbie and Laura within walking distance of Shelly Bay and within pedaling distance of us.

Uncle Arthur is a U. S. Foreign Service officer who has been so much in demand as a sort of accidental troubleshooter for the State Department that our children have had little opportunity to get acquainted with their only set of cousins. (Arthur is my lone sibling, and Barbara is an only child.)

During Uncle Arthur's first European assignment, Hungarian and Polish revolutionaries took up arms against the Russians, and Arthur was assigned to a refugee-processing center. He and the smog crisis were assigned to London at more or less the same time. He was posted to the Dominican Republic in time for their revolution. And not long after he and his family took up residence in the Renaissance city of Florence, the river Arno overflowed its banks, reaching its highest level since the sixteenth century. He was on home leave from his desk at the American embassy in The Hague at the time of his Bermuda holiday, and we crossed our fingers, fearing that brave Holland's dikes might collapse in his absence.

We had a very nice visit with Uncle Arthur's family, and the six cousins had their best-ever chance to get acquainted. Karen and Gretchen were given their first experiences at "sleeping over" with friends, and they argued shamelessly over whose turn was next.

Poor Käthe. She had six Breiskys to baby-sit while Uncle Arthur was on the island.

Our second vacation, in Enfield, came at summer's end and was made possible by our nonagenarian friend and former neighbor, Emma Stewart. We had written Mrs. Stewart that we would like very much to arrange a visit to see her and all our Enfield friends again, before our children forgot the faces and places that had been such a good and important influence on them. Mrs. Stewart made a mental note of that, and when she heard that Tom Barbour's replacement as the Congregational pastor, the Reverend Robert Lane, was taking his family to Maine for a few weeks, with the parsonage to be idle and probably no one to look after the cats, her Yankee nature would not permit her to rest until it was arranged that we would occupy the parsonage.

So we returned to Enfield in mid-August.

John was very nearly flattened by a truck before we had been in town twenty-four hours, as he dashed triumphantly across busy Enfield Street, bearing a plate of muffins Mrs. Stewart had baked especially for him, with blueberries picked that same morning.

Although Karen remembered most of "my ladies"—almost all of whom came to the parsonage to see what Bermuda had done for her—she was shy about saying so. A chocolate lollipop broke through her reserve, and she was rewarded with hugs and smiles each time she took a few independent steps on her knees or made such beautiful statements as, "I see the car. It's green."

The green car was the Kealey's big station wagon, which they had insisted we use while we were in Enfield.

"Are we stopping for Vaseline?" Gretchen wanted to know when we pulled into a service station in the big green wagon. Karen didn't know where or why we were stopping. We could get her to focus her eyes on a traffic signal if it was near enough, and if we sat at an intersection long enough—but she had not yet been able to recognize her surroundings from inside a car, so she certainly didn't know we were at a service station. She did, however, know that her sister's pronunciation was amiss.

"Vaseline?!" said Karen rather imperiously. "Vaseline is for *bottoms,* Gretchen. *Gasoline* is for cars."

We returned to Bermuda buoyed by the enthusiasm of all our old friends, who saw in Karen so many significant improvements that we had come to take for granted. And then it was time to say good-by to Käthe, who with her brother Paul had been looking after Whistling Winds and Doktor Pfeffer during our absence.

Gretchen told Käthe she had had a very nice time on her trip—especially with the parson's cats, "Princess" and "The White Tornado"—but she refused to admit that she had ever seen or heard of Enfield before, much less lived there.

CHAPTER XI

Word-Blind?

Apprehension.

Reading is apprehension—grasping the meaning of the written word.

Uneasiness is a form of apprehension.

Fearfulness is apprehension.

It is curious that this one word—apprehension—should have expressed both the problem (reading) and our reaction to the problem (uneasiness, fearfulness).

As John returned to school in the fall of 1969, we could not avoid looking ahead to the day when Karen would be required by society to begin competing with her peers, or be left behind. We knew that one September hence, Karen should be joining her brother in school.

Now, at the age of four and a half, she was barely able to scribble, but perhaps she could get along for a while without the skill to manage a pencil.

She had just learned knee-walking, but her mobility was improving steadily, and we believed she was on her way to walking on her feet.

Reading—that could be the real stumbling block. If a switched signal in Karen's brain wouldn't permit her eyes to read . . .

We had rejoiced in Karen's apprehension of stories we read to her, of concepts we explained, of new worlds we explored together. Would we—or she—one day come to accept her inability to apprehend the written word?

Words fail.

(Especially when eyes fail?)

Karen was not yet five years of age, and we were suffering anxieties because she could not find meaning in the particular form of hieroglyphics that English-speaking people favor.

Irrational?

Not when you're "on the program." Two years of age—Gretchen's age—is the best time to begin reading, says Glenn Doman. Gretchen was learning, and Karen, after more than a year's effort, had not yet mastered a single word.

Apprehension—fearfulness—was not with us every hour, or even every day, of course. Apprehension was only now and then. And apprehension was us, not Karen. Where there was Karen there was hope.

Correction.

Where there was Karen there was hope and *spirit*. (Karen to John, one day in early fall: "I didn't come to Bermuda to hear fussing!")

We moved in September 1969 from Whistling Winds to Eastleigh—from the east to the west end of Bermuda, from the crest of Cottage Hill to a sheltered cove off the Great Sound, plus a tree house for John, a program room for Karen, and close to a hundred banana trees to provide Saturday morning physical therapy for me.

What we lost in the swap were Arian Francis and Aunt Helen—all of our East End patterning ladies, in fact.

Nana and Grandpop came for moving day and to help with Karen's program during our settling-in period. It was to be their last visit for a while. They were retiring and moving to Clearwater, Florida, to escape Philadelphia's high taxes and low temperatures.

John was enrolled in the nearby Sandys Grammar School, and before he cracked his first book Barbara had lined up our first patterner, in the schoolyard. Going to the aid of a wailing waif who had misplaced his mother, Barbara had virtually collided with a friend from the past—Gloria Nichols Huf. The same Gloria Nichols who had been graduated from Philadelphia's Lincoln High with Barbara and had married classmate Ron Huf.

Swimming and gymnastics star Ron Huf had become Major Ron Huf, USMC, recently returned from Vietnam and serving as commanding officer of the small marine detachment assigned to the U. S. Naval Air Station Bermuda. Gloria said she would love to work with Karen and that she was certain she could bring along some navy wives as well.

As things turned out, Gloria Huf had the distinction of becoming the last of our patterning ladies. Barbara was told, in her autumn visit to Philadelphia that year, that she should call a halt to patterning and concentrate on visual and ladder work. The emphasis was to be on frequency—we were to make a greater effort to squeeze those eighteen brief programs into each twenty-four-hour day—and the new program would require more co-operation on Karen's part.

Almost any volunteer, Barbara had learned, could do a good job of patterning, but some lacked the inventiveness and enthusiasm necessary to bring out Karen's best efforts in those parts of the program that required her participation. So, more than grateful for past favors but with a sense of relief that she might manage her home once again without a daily string of visitors, Barbara decided to have a go at carrying out Karen's program alone, with me to do the "evening program" and to share the load on weekends.

Karen's eighteen daily programs were, theoretically, to require only five minutes each: a minute of cross-pattern crawling; three somersaults; half a minute each of hanging from a chinning bar, of flashlight constrictions, and of exposure to reading cards; and a minute of overhead ladder. But no more knee-walking under her ladder! She was to be on her feet now, with one of us hunched behind her, a hand on each hip. And just for good measure, we were told it would be a good idea to swing her occasionally from her feet.

Children with brain injury frequently have smaller measurements than most kids their age—smaller chests particularly, and thus less lung capacity. Karen was falling into this pattern of development, but the IAHP felt that getting her onto her feet and working frequently with the overhead ladder and chinning bar could halt or reverse this trend.

"Function determines structure," we were told, and a child can't be expected to develop as well as he should if he isn't functioning as he was meant to.

Before Karen left Philadelphia, an optometrist recommended by The Institutes prescribed glasses for her, to help correct her myopia. The optometrist was cautiously hopeful about Karen's eyes working better together, and focusing better, eventually. She would, however, very likely have to go through a stage of double vision before she could begin to focus effortlessly and with both eyes, he said, and Institutes-prescribed exercises ought to hasten that time.

Karen looked forward to getting her glasses, "so I can see better." She was, in fact, *determined* to see better. As soon as we had the prescription filled in Bermuda—with shatterproof plastic lenses—she peered into a car several steps away and announced grandly, "I see two children in that car. One is wearing a red dress and the other has a white shirt and blue pants."

Her description was accurate, and her parents were duly impressed—but Karen's determination and her desire to please impressed us more than her improved vision. The glasses were meant as an aid in distance vision; we knew she could see as well without them when it came to peering through the open window of a nearby car. And when we tried to determine whether her distance vision had been improved by the glasses, we were disappointed. We found she was still unable to focus on any of the boats and ships we saw from our second-floor veranda—white sails and brightly colored hulls well outlined against a plain backdrop of blue-green water.

We were given many clues to the mystery of Karen's vision, but the clues didn't lead to a solution.

Close-up stationary objects were becoming steadily easier for her to identify. Glancing at her dinner plate, she would now say, "Yum, corn for dinner," instead of "What's that yellow stuff?" Yet searching for a small object on our varicolored oriental rug remained a frustrating exercise for her, and she found the swirling images on our black-and-white TV screen totally baffling.

Our first family outing at the movies was a qualified success. The film was Walt Disney's *Cinderella,* and it was being shown on the largest movie screen in Bermuda. Karen sat on my lap and peered through her new glasses, as I alternately quizzed and coached her regarding the animated figures on the screen. She absorbed every detail I related, loved the talking mice and the fairy godmother, and Righty had no trouble fishing out handfuls of popcorn in the darkness.

"I like this movie," Karen declared at least three times. But we knew the images had moved too fast for her, even projected on a fifty-foot-wide screen. Karen had been laughing and squealing with delight, but it was a sort of delayed-reaction laughter, in response to the laughter of the other children around her as much as to what was happening on the screen.

The scene took me back to a poignant memory from my own growing-up years. My brother and I had been sent to boarding school in Baltimore for a time after our mother died. Saturday afternoon outings were a reward for respectable behavior, and we thirteen-year-olds were permitted to strike out on our own. On several of those long-ago Saturdays I had been treated to not one but two movies by a well-to-do, totally deaf classmate who found me the most satisfactory movie partner from our dorm because my narration had proved the easiest to lip-read in a darkened theater. Sitting in Bermuda's Rosebank Theatre with Karen on my lap, I thought back to a Saturday afternoon at the Keith's Theatre in downtown Baltimore, where my deafened friend Richard jabbed me repeatedly during *The Wolf Man* to ask, "What did he say? . . . What did he say?"

Richard enjoyed *watching* movies more than anyone I've

ever met. Karen proved a very good movie *listener*, and now I was being called on to explain "What are they doing?" rather than "What did he say?" But movies are more fun to watch than to listen to, and I suspected Karen's enthusiasm resulted as much from the popcorn and the adventure of it all as from the movie itself.

Records and picture books were Karen's forte. She listened harder than her brother and sister to the children's records we played during her program and usually learned the lyrics and stories faster. She listened to every word, and if she didn't understand a word, she would pause at mid-ladder to ask its meaning. (From our *Born Free* record: "What does 'astound' mean?" "It means to surprise." "I like surprises.")

Big books with big pictures were great fun, too, because these pictures, unlike TV pictures, held still. If the stories in these picture books were short and involved little girls, Karen could virtually commit the text to memory, and by turning pages and reciting memorized words she could give the illusion of reading. She would announce, in fact, that "I'm reading," and could fool anyone who didn't know the limitations of her eyesight.

In truth, Karen couldn't read a word.

But while we were groping for explanations and solutions regarding Karen's inability to find meaning in printed letters and numbers, we witnessed encouraging improvement in the ability of her brain to command obedience from her right hand and from her legs.

"Righty" experienced no difficulty reaching into bowls and platefuls of candy on Halloween night when we took the girls out trick-or-treating for the first time. Philadelphia friends Arnold and Elisabeth Nicholson were staying with us that week. Elisabeth dressed in a witch's costume and chased us all out of the house so that both Barbara and I could make the rounds with a cowboy named John, who could manage very nicely by himself, and with cowgirls named Karen and Gretchen (she was a "Chinese cowgirl," actually), who wished to be carried.

Late that fall Righty scored a number of minor triumphs which wouldn't find their way into most family histories but were more than worthy of being recorded in ours.

He (Righty, Karen claims, is a he) learned to depress the flushing handle on our toilet.

He also summoned enough strength in his forefinger—it was a matter of isolating and applying the strength in a limited area, really—to sock one key at a time on my typewriter, the key of his choice most times, and actually make a black impression on a piece of paper. (Back in Enfield, Righty had been able to press the space bar sufficient times to make the bell ring, even though Karen was virtually sightless. But to find that little *k* key and to strike it hard enough to make a *k* on the paper—that was something!)

A month later, we found Karen on the floor of the girls' room, toying with the control knob of the electric space heaters we island-dwellers install to combat winter's-evening chills and that bane of all denizens of the tropics and subtropics, mildew. The knob that had captured Karen's interest was a thermostatic control, and I explained to her that it was only slightly more difficult to manipulate than the transistor radio dial, that if she turned it to the right, the heat would come on, and that if she turned it far enough to the left, the heat would be shut off.

She tinkered with it and soon found that merely by placing a finger on the top of the knob and pushing to the right she could turn on the heat, whereas turning it to the left, with Righty, required her to grasp the knob with her fingers.

"Okay, Righty old boy," I said. "I'm going to turn the heater on. Now, if you can turn it off by yourself, Karen earns a penny."

Karen earned the penny in two minutes flat, requested her purse, deposited the penny, crept and knee-walked over to her dresser, dropped the purse into the bottom drawer, and announced somewhat ominously, "I'm gonna earn a *lotta* money."

Sure enough, no sooner was Karen out of bed the next morning than Righty was tugging at the handle of that bottom drawer where the money was stored. Barbara interrupted the proceedings at that juncture to point out that while Daddy's motivation and Righty's enthusiasm were to be applauded, perhaps we could find some more purposeful project, because parents should not really encourage children to adjust all the heater thermostats in the house and expect to be rewarded for it.

Righty's improved function was, of course, a result of all the work Barbara and Karen were doing with the overhead ladder and with the bedroom chinning bar. Karen became proficient enough to grasp the chinning bar or a pole and to swing for several seconds at a time, supporting her own weight, if we gave Lefty some slight assistance.

Her knee-walking skill progressed slowly but surely, so that she could take more and more steps before falling forward onto her hands—but even before she became a competent knee-walker she discovered she could "jump" on her knees. It had never occurred to John and Gretchen to jump around on their knees, so, of course, Karen proclaimed herself the best knee-jumper in the family, if not in the western parishes of Bermuda.

She also became the family's best storyteller.

Once upon a dinner, in December 1969, in a cheerful old house called Eastleigh, there was a four-and-three-quarter-year-old girl named Karen, who having finished her lemon Jell-O and Peek Freans biscuits, commenced regaling her family with a tale about animals and children, and the story went on and on and on and and on. We thought it would never end.

We applauded—John and Gretchen with some slight urging from their parents—and advised Karen that she was no doubt the best storyteller in the family.

She was, really. I don't remember that first drawn-out story, but I remember being impressed that it was imaginative and rather rich in detail and quite the longest story I had ever heard from anyone Karen's age.

In any case, encouragement was all Karen needed. Bedtime remained the time when parents were required to come up with an entertaining story, but Karen assumed responsibility for wake-up-time entertainment on Saturday and Sunday mornings. "Now listen to this story" were likely to be the first words we heard from her on a weekend morning. I won't say that each story was better than the last (we storytellers have our ups and downs, after all), but they did demonstrate pride, persistence, and a growing awareness of the world around her.

Karen *remains* the best storyteller in the family. Why? Because of her skill as a listener, she may have absorbed the art of storytelling better than most children. Living in a circumscribed world may have made her more introspective, more likely to invent fanciful tales of characters with limitless skills. Her particular combination of genes and chromosomes may also have something to do with her storytelling ability. But genes and introspection and listening skills can only be a part of the answer. I'm certain Karen has persisted in her endlessly intriguing (sometimes just plain endless) stories because she has had a championship to uphold and defend. Because she had been told she was the best storyteller, she was determined to *remain* the best storyteller.

She also gave us a few clues, that fall and early winter, that she was determined to walk away from her overhead ladder.

We installed a rope ladder at one end of the overhead ladder so that she could pull herself into a standing position. She soon mastered that and promised us "six good ladders"—walking the length of her ladder, hand over hand, six times in succession—by Christmas. When Christmas arrived, she was able to double the promised six—and to walk a few dozen hesitant steps in the supermarket by holding onto the handle of the shopping basket.

Christmas 1969 was the Christmas of Ronnie and Alastair.

We had signed up to invite a pair of seamen from the frigate H.M.S. *Mohawk* to have dinner with us on Christmas Day—a Royal Navy frigate is invariably tied up in Hamilton Harbour over the holidays, and her men invited into Bermudian homes—and had specified only that we be sent "men who aren't allergic to small children." We got Ronnie Douglas and Alastair Morrison, who proved themselves anything but ordinary seamen.

Ronnie and Alastair came for Christmas dinner and stayed, off and on, until . . . March, I think it was. Her Majesty's Ship *Mohawk* developed some propeller problems, requiring a rather lengthy layover at H. M. Dockyard, and when she finally put out to sea again, it was for maneuvers in the Caribbean, with a couple of calls at Bermuda scheduled before her return to the United Kingdom.

Ronnie and Alastair were Scotsmen—Ronnie from the mining town of Loanhead, outside Edinburgh; Alastair from Muthill, a small village set among the sprawling sheep farms of Perthshire. Both were men of few words, scotch sippers, endlessly patient at playing children's games, and more than a little grateful for an occasional night in our spare room, away from the *Mohawk*'s throbbing engines. Ronnie was angular, wryly engaging, devoted to a Loanhead lass named Kathleen, and his shoulders were just the right size for carrying a Gretchen. Alastair was sandy-haired and rawboned—Scottish-looking, he was—and partial to bulky sweaters, to Margaret Deacons of Crieff, and to Karen Breisky of Somerset.

Ronnie helped Gretchen arrange the furniture in the two-story, open-walled dollhouse Barbara and I (mostly Barbara) had built as a Christmas gift for the girls, and Alastair dressed Karen's chinning bar in bright stripes to give Karen an additional visual game to play while she was doing her monkey business.

"Me and Alastair thinked it up," Karen announced when the chinning-bar project had been completed.

Christmas 1967: Karen doing her first assistive crawling, pushing with a leg against our hands, and just able to see the beam of a D-cell flashlight in the dark.

Christmas 1968: Karen creeping on hands and knees to an "I think I can" cadence, mastering the art of balancing herself on her knees, able to see her new doll but not distant objects.

Christmas 1969: Karen walking hand-over-hand under her overhead ladder and able to take a few steps when given a broom handle or a shopping-cart handle to grasp. Admiring the blue ocean through new spectacles. Producing a crude circle on her side of the double blackboard she shared with Gretchen—her first serious effort at producing anything other than a scribble. Telling endless stories. Memorizing simple storybooks—text and pictures—but still unable to decipher one-dimensional pictures until they had been explained thoroughly, and totally unable to comprehend the written word, yet mature enough to say, wistfully but with no bitterness or even unhappiness, "I wish I could get rid of these eyes and have Gretchen's eyes."

Karen's musical gift that Christmas was a push-button harmonica horn, which she managed to toot after some frustration by holding the instrument against her left shoulder with her left hand while pressing the colored buttons with Righty.

"Put that in my book," she insisted immediately, "about pressing the buttons and making music."

I had frequently told Karen that the little notebooks I kept on her progress would be hers one day, so that she could have a record of all the things she had worked so hard to accomplish, but this was the first time she had suggested that an entry be made.

I was, in fact, making Christmas 1969 notes in "Karen's book" until January 5, 1970. We had taken the children to see the Nativity pageant at St. James Church in Somerset and had arrived early so that we might seat Karen and Gretchen in the front pew. Even so, it hadn't seemed that Karen had seen or understood much of what happened on the dimly lit chancel, ten or twelve feet in front of her, except when Barbara or I had whispered explanations. Early in the new year, however, I was able to record that she had seen more than we had realized:

> Monday, January 5—Christmas is behind us, but the melodies linger on. Karen requested the "Silent Night" record album while she was doing her ladder tonight, and when "O Little Town of Bethlehem" was played, she asked, "What's that song, Daddy?"

" 'O Little Town of Bethlehem' is the name," I said. "Jesus was born in a town called Bethlehem. You were born in a city called Hartford."

"Oh," was all she said until she reached the end of her ladder, and then, "Daddy?"

"What, Karen?"

"Why didn't they put their shoes on?"

"Why didn't who put their shoes on?"

"The shepherds."

Meaning, of course, the Christmas pageant shepherds, whose bare feet Karen had noted but hadn't bothered to call to our attention previously.

Four days later I contributed something of Barbara's to "Karen's book"—a note I found on my dresser when I returned home from work.

If Barbara is really angry, she lets off steam and thereby puts the anger behind her. If she's especially happy, or especially worried, she writes a note—and this time she was worried:

Bill—

I can't teach Karen to read with these word signs or with any sight system. Maybe if she learned by some sort of listening approach—can't imagine what.

Gretchen now has four words down pat and is anxious to go on. When do I do it? With Karen, so she can suffer more defeats?

The Doman book says not to go ahead until you're sure that the child has understood the difference between "Mommy" and "Daddy" signs. Karen doesn't. And she can't begin to tell "nose" from "hand."

I'm sick.

I stared a long time at that note before we talked about it. It seemed obvious that The Institutes had a lot to learn about Karen's vision, but it seemed equally obvious that her general progress indicated we were doing something right and that we should continue to have faith in the IAHP theory that progress in one area will stimulate progress in another.

Of course, Karen came through with an achievement that

answered Barbara's anguish far better than my words could. Just two days after Barbara wrote her note, Karen experienced the exquisite joy of standing alone. She was doing her overhead ladder, and at ladder's end, instead of grasping the rope ladder and letting herself down to the floor, she simply released both her hands and stood still, feet apart, holding onto nothing but faith and balancing herself for what seemed an age and a half, but was in fact about ten seconds.

"Again!" she said.

She insisted on trying this balancing act every time she did her ladder work that day, and by the end of the afternoon she was able to stand alone under her ladder for a full half a minute. She was able to sense, furthermore, when she was about to lose her balance. When she fell forward, she would catch herself by grasping a rung with one or both hands, and when she fell backward, she squealed with delight at the sensation of falling and trusted that someone would be there with open arms.

Our late-January 1970 appointment at The Institutes was to have been my turn—my first Philadelphia trip since we moved to Bermuda—and because Nana and Grandpop had abandoned Philadelphia in favor of Florida, I begged room and board from our friends the Nicholsons, who had been such a hit with Karen on Halloween.

The portrait of Elisabeth Nicholson's white-bearded, severe-looking grandfather, "Mr. Berryhill," on the stairs leading to the room where Karen would sleep, seemed almost as frightening a figure as Mrs. Nicholson's Halloween witch, and Karen had to be assured that it was safe for her to go to sleep. But on her way downstairs to breakfast the next morning, she sang out cheerily, "Good morning, Mr. Berryhill!"

On previous visits to The Institutes, Karen had succeeded in half convincing Sandy Brown that she was beginning to learn her word signs—but Barbara and I remained unconvinced. Sandy would discuss a few words with Karen—"Mommy," "ball," and "cup"—then spread the signs on the floor and ask Karen to touch the one that said "ball." Karen seemed to do her best guessing when Sandy was doing the asking—but guessing it was, and when I took Karen to Philadelphia in January, Sandy agreed that Karen seemed to be making no progress in her reading program.

"If Karen were ten," Sandy said, "I would almost have to admit that she is word-blind. But she's not ten, and I think we had better try a new approach."

Sandy told me of a technique that had recently worked for a youngster whose vision problem seemed very much like Karen's. The technique had been developed not by The Institutes, but by the youngster's father, a Millersburg, Pennsylvania, printshop proprietor named Robert Kurtz. He had made 35-mm slides of printed words, then had produced reverse slides so that white letters were displayed against a black background. The slides were projected in a totally dark room.

We phoned Millersburg there and then, and asked Mr. Kurtz if he would have a photo lab make a duplicate set of his slides for Karen. He said he would be very happy to, and wished us luck.

During the same visit, another member of The Institutes staff suggested yet another technique for getting Karen to read: Keep her flat on her back when she's looking at her word signs.

I asked IAHP staff members about Karen's complaint that she was unable to close her eyes voluntarily and could get no answer other than "That's a new one on me." The Institutes seemed to be groping as far as Karen's vision was concerned, but we were more than willing to keep trying as long as they were. Until the slides arrived from Millersburg, we would continue the word-sign program, with Karen on her back.

CHAPTER XII

Some Brand-new Things from Karen Breisky

All good humor has a basis in truth, and I suspect that few experts in matters neurological can resist smiling at the element of truth in comic Tom Poston's Lesson No. 1 on brain function.

"The most important function of the brain," says Poston, "is to tell the feet when it's time to run."

I'm certain Karen's brain tried to suggest to her feet that it was time to run the first time her eyes were able to verify to her brain, via visual feedback, what running was all about. But in Karen's case, the feet weren't listening to the brain. The brain was talking, but there was a bad connection—some strong interference on the line or a crossed wire—and those feet just weren't getting the message.

On Lincoln's Birthday 1970, however, Karen's brain sent out a message that directed her feet to take a few steps away from her ladder, with a minimum of support.

The Institutes had instructed us to tie lengths of rope, knotted at given intervals, to the rungs on Karen's overhead ladder. She was to push down on the ropes, making them taut, when she felt unsteady, and to raise her hands, making the ropes slack, when she felt secure enough to practice balance. Sandy Brown predicted that Karen would walk away from those ropes—and Karen began to do just that on Abraham Lincoln's birthday.

That mid-February walk took place in the girls' bedroom, where Barbara and Karen were using a chinning bar for walking practice. The chinning bar was nothing more than a piece of pipe resting on notched blocks of wood we had nailed on the jambs of the doorway leading to John's room. Barbara had attached ropes to the chinning bar so Karen could do some practice-walking under it, but on Lincoln's Birthday she removed the bar, held it in front of Karen, and let her grasp it lightly—just enough for balance—and told Karen to step out. Karen responded with a series of rigid, puppetlike but enormously satisfying steps.

No sooner had I arrived home from work that evening than I received my instructions from Karen. "Put it in my book," she said. "A brand-new thing from Karen Breisky." And she told me of the historic steps.

After almost three more weeks of using ropes, rungs and chinning bars for balance, I told Karen just before dinner one evening, "We haven't had anything to put in your book for a while. Isn't it time you did something new?"

Karen agreed it was high time, but said she couldn't think of anything to try; so I suggested, "How about getting your balance, then taking a couple of steps without holding onto anything?"

Her eyes widened as she considered this enormous suggestion; then suddenly she sucked in her breath, took three quick, brave steps, and fell into my arms.

Q. When does a baby step become a giant step?

A. When you have lost your ability to creep, much less walk, and have spent three long years undoing the damage.

There was joy in Eastleigh that evening. The thousands of hours of patterning, assistive crawling, crawling, creeping, knee-walking and somersaulting were paying a large dividend. Karen repeated her three-step performance four times during the evening, and we all went to bed very happy indeed.

Not to be outdone, Gretchen upstaged Karen's performance with a walking demonstration that very nearly became a matter for the police.

Gretchen had been enrolled in a morning program at a

neighborhood nursery school a few weeks earlier, to allow Barbara to concentrate on Karen's program. Gretch was beginning to demand more attention, and Barbara's solution was to concentrate on Karen's program in the mornings so that she could give the girls equal shares of attention in the afternoons.

The first few weeks went very well, but one drizzly winter's day Gretchen apparently made up her mind that she had had enough, or at least that she needed a day off. Somehow she slipped out of her class unnoticed. A head count was taken moments later—no Gretchen!—and the building and grounds of the nursery were searched frantically. Not a clue was found. Meanwhile the owner of the school had been located by telephone, the location of Gretchen's home determined, and a pursuit car dispatched.

Our three-year-old Marco Polo was found heading south on Sound View Road, in the direction of our driveway. Throughout the period of reasoning, imploring and interrogating that followed, she maintained a stony silence, declining to discuss the matter with anyone.

Karen, aged almost five, had taken three steps and been warmly praised; Gretchen, aged three, had hiked home from school in the rain, unescorted, and was rewarded with a runny nose and a scolding. Justice, wheresoever art thou?

Arriving at Eastleigh about half an hour ahead of Gretchen that day was a package of hope—Mr. Kurtz's slides from Millersburg. That evening we converted the nine-foot-wide closet in the downstairs guest room into a projection room. My slide projector was set up on a step stool at one end of the closet, and the word slides were projected onto the opposite wall. We began with the words "bread" and "ball."

Karen showed immediate enthusiasm for the game, even though Lesson No. 1 didn't get through to her. We knew from experience, however, that she would try her best to convince us that she could read, just as she had on the floor of Sandy

Brown's office at The Institutes, when Sandy had spread out the words "apple," "banana" and "orange."

"Give me 'banana,' Karen," Sandy had requested.

Karen had reached out in a tentative way, touched the "apple" sign, and said, when we didn't praise her immediately, "That's not banana."

"I know," Sandy had declared. "Do you know which one *is* banana?"

"Daddy knows," Karen replied.

The first two weeks of projecting "ball," "bread," "telephone," "water," "jelly," "bag," "paper" and "potato" on the wall of the guest-room closet were inconclusive. We limited ourselves to a small selection of words, describing the letters, spelling them out, using them in sentences, playing word games with them, but could not really tell whether we were getting through or not. Reading sessions on her back had seemed a failure, and we could only say of the word slides that Karen showed more enthusiasm for them than for any previous method of reading instruction.

"Telephone" was the first word she was able to identify with any consistency—but for the simple reason that it was the longest word we presented her.

She identified "water" correctly on several occasions, but if she really could read "water," why could she never identify either of the simplest words in the inventory we had selected —"ball" and "bag"?

"What's this word, Karen?"

Pause. Then, "Spell it."

"*B-a-l-l.*"

"Ball!"

"Good, Karen." (Good she remembered hearing that *b-a-l-l* spells ball, but not good that she was unable to identify the word by sight.)

Nana Liz came to see us in early April. It was her first visit in a year. "When you come back, I'm gonna walk for you," Karen had promised. And she kept that promise, walking a record-breaking eleven unassisted steps two days after Nana Liz's arrival.

Karen took a bow for the walking performance, but when she accomplished her first unassisted somersault on the same day, she insisted that our old friend Geraldine had been responsible. Good old Geraldine. How like her to pitch in, just when Karen seemed to be getting bored with her somersaulting lessons.

The somersaulting success demonstrated a lesson that we've observed over and over again with Karen: Practice makes perfect, and perfect makes enthusiasm. It had taken months of intensive and monotonous practice before Karen could do her first somersault, but once she had managed to flip herself over without helping hands, there was no stopping her. Somersaulting became an exciting, fulfilling, joyous activity.

Success in one area stimulates and reinforces success in other areas, we had been told repeatedly in Philadelphia, and we were inclined to go along with that theory when the long-awaited breakthrough in reading finally came, following on the heels of the walking and somersaulting achievements.

"What's that letter on the right?" Karen asked, some six weeks after her word slides arrived, when we flashed "bag" on the closet wall.

"G."

"Bag."

"Great. See if you can get this next one."

"Water?"

"Beautiful! . . . And this one?"

"I see a *j* with a moon over it. . . . Jelly!"

"Wonderful. Now here comes a hard one."

Ten seconds' silence. "Is that a word you can eat?"

"Yes."

"Well, it's not 'jelly.' " Is it 'potato'?"

"It's potato, all right. Were you guessing or did you really know?"

"I knew it wasn't 'bread' or 'jelly.' "

Another "brand-new thing from Karen Breisky"! Hers was a hesitant, deductive kind of reading, but it was (to borrow from the Chinese) a very great leap forward indeed.

Karen could walk—thirteen steps. Karen could read—"jelly," "bag," and "telephone," projected on a closet wall. With these hurdles cleared, Barbara and I decided we could afford to take a break; so after getting Nana and Grandpop to say yes, they would be delighted to take over Karen's program and keep an eye on Gretchen the wanderer, we wrote to Ted and Rosemary Tedesco, out in Boulder, Colorado, to announce, "We'll see you in Venice."

The Tedescos had asked us shortly after the first of the year if we would rendezvous in Europe with them in mid-May. We had wanted to go—to see the Tedescos, to see Uncle Arthur's family in The Hague, and to see London—and while we had studied a few travel guides and tantalized ourselves mercilessly, we had strong reservations about leaving while Karen remained on the verge of so many achievements. We canceled those reservations, however, when Karen achieved her breakthroughs in walking and reading.

Karen's self-confidence, meanwhile, was keeping pace with her achievements. A pouting lower lip had remained her stormy-weather signal, but her pouting spells, never a problem, were becoming less frequent and of shorter duration.

One morning after suffering an alleged slight at the hands of her mother, she ran off to her room on her knees, presumably to bawl. But she returned shortly, and proudly, announcing, "Mommy, I got control of myself."

The girls were graduated from the nursery room at Sunday school in early April and put in a primary class. Sunday school became an eagerly awaited part of the week for Karen—her first group activity and thus an important social outing. It didn't seem to bother her that we had to lift her into a chair at the table and had to put her collection money in front of her, where she could reach it, rather than leaving it in her purse, and that she couldn't handle crayons or scissors. It didn't matter that she needed more help than the other children; Karen was grateful for the degree of participation she had achieved. She was proudly clutching a Bible-lesson illustration when we picked her up after that first lesson, and she announced to us, "The teacher said it was okay to take Jesus home." Amen.

Karen learned to recite her ABC's that spring. And she learned to use a toothpick.

Karen has sat at my right at the dinner table for as long as I can remember, and it has become my job to fetch toothpicks as well as to cut her meat, help load her spoon, and butter her bread. But there came a day, during a chicken dinner in early April 1970, when I made my usual offer to locate and remove an irritating morsel of meat with a toothpick and she insisted, "No. I'll do it myself." She succeeded immediately, and we recorded another minor achievement. Not her most ladylike performance, by a long shot, but one of her most dexterous.

"Am I five now?" Karen asked when her birthday dawned. She knew the answer, yet there was uncertainty in her voice.

"Yes, Karen."

"Then why can't I walk?"

Six to twelve steps at a time, to her way of thinking, wasn't real walking. Obviously a recent and casual remark, "When you're five and can walk . . . ," had meant to her that something magic was going to happen on April 27. But she was quick to accept Barbara's reasoning that inasmuch as she had started walking when she was four, and would have 365 days of being five, the prophecy would surely be fulfilled.

Barbara and I had gone birthday shopping for Karen on the same day, Barbara in Philadelphia and myself in Bermuda, in search, as always, for a toy or game that would challenge but not frustrate her and that might help develop her hand-eye co-ordination. We are so accustomed to operating on the same frequency, Karen-wise, that we weren't really surprised to discover that each of us had bought the same gift—a wooden puzzle.

We also bought her a musical typewriter with color-coded keys the size of quarters, and I bought myself an 8-mm movie camera. Now that Karen was becoming, as she put it, "a walking girl," mere photographs could no longer do justice to her progress.

I don't suppose we ever will shoot a roll of film that will score higher on the applause charts than our very first one. Sharing featured roles with our family on that roll were a young New York attorney and his wife, Ed and Joanne Carroll. Ed, who volunteered his services as cameraman for Scene 1, played a lead role in Scene 2.

Ed and Joanne had flown down to Bermuda especially to see Karen, after hearing her story through a friend who had met one of our patterning ladies on a visit to Bermuda. They hoped to see—and wanted to believe—that methods which had helped Karen might be applied to their daughter Sue Lynn, who had been stricken at very nearly the same age, in very nearly the same way.

Scene 1: The dining room at Eastleigh. A dish of orange hibiscus blossoms brightens the table. At the head of the table is the father of the family, white teeth gleaming beneath untidy black moustache. To his right, also gleaming, is the guest of honor, Karen, five years old today. Standing on each side of her, properly outfitted in homemade party hats and eyes fixed on the kitchen door, are brother John and sister Gretchen. Enter the source of excitement—mother bearing cake with five pink candles. Following on her heels is Nana Liz; she is thin, wears her gray hair close-cropped, has a gaily patterned sweater-jacket over her shoulders. Everyone is singing a boisterous rendition of "Happy Birthday to You." The children can't take their eyes off the cake; Barbara and Nana Liz are looking not at the cake, but at the birthday girl, and you can read in their eyes and in the creases in their faces a sense of joy born of gratitude that Karen is so much a part of things on her fifth birthday. Karen's arms are bent at the elbow, her hands overlapping one another in front of her chest— a characteristic gesture when she is tense with joy. The cake is placed before her, and Barbara must wag a finger at golden-haired

Gretchen, who has leaned forward toward the candles and drawn a deep breath. Gretchen retreats, and Karen begins to huff and puff at the candles. The camera zooms in on the huffing and puffing, and after six reasonably well aimed puffs from Karen and one sudden assist from the sidelines by John, the candles are extinguished. Amid a round of applause Gretchen's right hand darts out. A forefinger has been detected by Karen in the act of sampling the icing and is retreating toward Gretchen's mouth when there is an abrupt cut to . . .

Scene 2: Later that April afternoon, on the upper lawn of Eastleigh. The oleander is in full bloom and six people—four large and two small—have formed a circle in front of the papaw tree. The small people, Karen and Gretchen, have joined hands with their mother, Nana Liz, and Ed and Joanne Carroll. They are singing "Ring Around a Rosy" and, taking little sideways steps, moving slowly counterclockwise. After eight steps it's "all fall down" time, and the circle suddenly collapses. All fall to their knees except Ed Carroll and Karen, who land on their bottoms. On the second go-round, Karen is given the role of "Rosy," and the others form a circle around her. Joanne reaches out to balance her when she begins to teeter, and when all-fall-down time comes, Karen falls toward Ed, who gives her a squeeze, then plants her on her feet again. The scene ends with Ed and Joanne facing one another. Ed is on his knees, arms outstretched. Joanne is standing half a dozen baby steps away; Karen is propped up against her, and Gretchen stands alongside. At a signal Karen—knee socks beginning to droop, face radiant—steps out toward Ed. Her steps are small but quick, her arms held high for balance, and a shoulder dips each time a leg reaches out, with the result that her arms are swinging her torso from side to side as her legs carry her forward. It's a tiring way to walk, and she throws herself into Ed's arms. Gretchen has been observing the demonstration with mixed emotions, and in the instant that Joanne begins to applaud, Gretchen turns and wraps her arms tightly around the skirt of Joanne's red dress, in a gesture that says, "I'm here, too."

We think often about the Carrolls and about the spiritual bond we felt even before we met. Their Sue Lynn had suffered a bout with epiglottitis at two, just as Karen had, and

had been carelessly attended in the intensive-care unit of a
New York City hospital. Her endotracheal tube had become
clogged with mucus, and after almost suffocating to death she
had been left with massive brain damage—speechless, immobile,
sightless.

A friend of the Carrolls', having heard our story from a
patterner, phoned me from the Bermuda airport to relate this
story which so closely paralleled our own, asked some questions
about The Institutes, and gave me the Carrolls' address in
Riverdale, just across the Harlem River from Manhattan.

Meanwhile Ed and Joanne Carroll had made a novena for
little Sue Lynn. They hoped that after those nine days of
devotions their prayers would somehow be answered—and on
the ninth day a postman delivered to their mailbox Barbara's
long and encouraging letter about Karen's tragedy and triumphs,
with the suggestion that they fly down for a visit.

The Carrolls phoned us almost immediately and set a date.
Sue Lynn, we learned, had been stricken half a year earlier
and had made no visible progress since then. She seemed
unable to respond or to express herself in any way.

Karen was more than happy to put on her best demonstration during the weekend that the Carrolls were with us—and
the Carrolls decided to apply to The Institutes. As they left,
grateful to Karen for renewing their hope, Karen expressed a
wish that Sue Lynn would "get a program, so she can get
better—like me."

Nana Liz flew back to New York with the Carrolls, but
our guest room was idle for very few days before Nana and
Grandpop arrived, to visit with us and then to mind the girls
while Barbara, John and I were off for three weeks in England
and on the Continent.

Nana helped us discover in her first few days with us that
the secret of successful walking with Karen was to assign her a
destination and to stand directly behind her rather than in

front of her. That way she had a goal, and she was not so tempted to reach out for a helping hand.

A week before our flight to London, Karen walked seventeen steps across the playroom to her Nana, and for the first time she had the confidence not to rush headlong but to pause after a few steps and regain her balance.

Her closet reading went so well that we soon needed additional word slides. Two friends at the Bermuda News Bureau photographed a series of single words on black-and-white film with a 35-mm camera, made 8″ by 10″ prints of each, then mounted the negatives as slides so that I could project them. The new slides were a shade more difficult—white letters against a gray rather than a black background—but Karen adapted quickly, and we had a hunch that our walking and somer-saulting daughter would be reading the 8″ by 10″ printed words with her Nana before we got back from our trip.

CHAPTER XIII

Time Off for Good Behavior

or

Europe on a Mere $6.63 a Day (Including Dry Cleaning, But Not Room, Meals, or Transportation)

The plan: to fly to London with John, to see where the Queen of British Bermuda lived, and to take in those sights that would appeal the most to an almost-seven-year-old boy; then go on to Holland to deposit John in The Hague, in the household of Uncle Arthur, Aunt Marlene, Doug, Debbie and Laura. While John was getting reacquainted with his cousins, Barbara and I would join Ted and Rosemary Tedesco for a week of touring from Venice to Innsbruck.

The object: to give ourselves some time off for good behavior—Karen's good behavior. To get a bit of perspective. To gawk at great mountains and to laugh at inconsequential things.

The problem: Critics of The Institutes for the Achievement of Human Potential are correct on one score: Parents of kids who are on the program really do feel guilty when they're not utilizing a portion of every waking hour on some activity that might help nudge their child up the ladder of neurological organization.

The solution to the problem: Barbara's mother, tireless where

Karen is concerned, patient, loving, strong, quick to praise, and determined to help Karen achieve her best. I think Karen inherited quite a bit of her strength of character from her Nana.

Certainly Karen and Gretchen didn't make us feel at all guilty about abandoning them for a fortnight and a half. As we descended our driveway in the early evening of May 9, in a taxi headed for the airport, the girls were waving good-by and shouting demands that we have a good time. As far as they were concerned, they had the better part of the deal; anyone who would go on a trip while Nana and Grandpop were visiting must be slightly daft.

We hadn't been away from Karen for as much as a night since her hospitalization in Hartford three years earlier, so I asked Nana to jot down a few highlights of life at Eastleigh —particularly Karen's doings—during our absence. Her journal filled only one sheet of paper, but it was reassuring enough, full enough of the joy of life, to make us realize we needn't have been in a hurry to get back.

May 12: Karen succeeded in blowing bubbles with her bubble pipe today. "I'm having a great time," she said.
London with John was buying a sixpence sack of peanuts to feed the famished pigeons at Westminster Bridge and a sack of grapes on Piccadilly Circus to feed ourselves; taking movies of mother and son running in the rain under an umbrella alongside the Queen's Horse Guards; shopping for a tam for a small boy whose ears were getting cold; Fleet Street friends treating us to "beef and pud" at Ye Olde Cheshire Cheese pub ("Re-built 1667"); wide-eyed curiosity as to how the Bloody Tower earned its name; lemon ice between acts of *Fiddler on the Roof* at Her Majesty's Theatre; and Barbara promising to rendezvous at the West Side Terminal on Cromwell Road if we would please let her squeeze in a half-hour shopping trip at Harrod's whilst father and son returned to the hotel to pack and check out.

May 13: Karen is reading the word signs made from the slides! She can read "boat," "blue," "Gretchen," "walk" and "see."

Uncle Arthur was waiting for us under a Coca-Cola sign at Amsterdam's Schiphol Airport. We drove to van Soutelande-laan in The Hague, with a detour to Keukenhof to see the tulips and hyacinths. We told John to enjoy himself while we were away, but advised Aunt Marlene to ignore his suggestion that a pair of wooden shoes would make the best possible replacement for the slippers he had left under his bed in London.

May 14: Karen asked if she could help polish the coffee table "for Mommy," and insisted when she was tucked in for the night, "Nana, you go to bed early so you can get your rest."

Venice.

Bumped into the Tedescos on Calle dei Fabri, en route to our hotel. Welcomed one another noisily, extravagantly, Italian-style. Awed by the Piazza San Marco—and by the report that the pigeon population there was being fed birth control pills. Sobered by how quickly one can be separated from 1000 lire. (To see the sights from atop the Campanile: 300 lire for the elevator ride, 100 lire to peer through the telescope, another 100 for a recorded "explanation" of what you're looking at through the telescope.) Delighted by our discovery of Peggy Guggenheim's little museum and its Venetian garden. Ashamed of ourselves for departing Venice without experiencing a gondola ride ("*Six thousand lire?!* We'll give you four thousand," said Ted in Berlitz Italian. Undiluted scorn from the gondolier. "Four thousand doesn't buy spaghetti.")

May 18: Grandpop became annoyed because Karen was toying with her food during dinner. He retreated to the kitchen, and when he reappeared and stood in the doorway, Karen declared, "Here comes the judge!"

Driving from Venice to Klagenfurt, capital of the Austrian

province of Carinthia, Barbara, Ted and Rosemary voted down my plan to "go to Yugoslavia for lunch"—but capitulated when they saw what a sore loser I was going to be.

Lunch was a wine and goat-cheese stop on a hillside outside Ljubljana. Supper was a reunion with my Austrian cousin Alice and her husband, Ingomar, in Klagenfurt.

We were nourished by Mozart and venison steak in Salzburg—then it was on to Innsbruck. There a German-born economics professor gave us a tour of the city and led us to the University of Innsbruck physics building, where a bas-relief likeness of Grandpa Hess—Nana Liz's late husband—adorns one wall of the lobby.

"In England," our Innsbruck guide told us, "you can do *anything* unless it is expressly forbidden. In Germany, everything is *verboten* unless there is a law permitting it. But here in Austria—while everything is *verboten*, people do it anyway."

It was an amusing theory, but like many theories put forward by economists these days, it was not entirely borne out by events. In Innsbruck's Hotel Tyrol, a gloriously proportioned chambermaid demonstrated that certain forms of behavior are *not* tolerated in laissez-faire Austria, economics professors' theories to the contrary.

The plumbing fixtures in the Tyrol were the last word in gleaming efficiency, but there being nothing else to support a coat hanger around our king-sized tub, I hung my drip-dry Hathaway shirt on the pull chain alongside the exhaust vent. Almost instantly, following a rattling of keys in the hallway, that splendid chambermaid burst into the room, sized up the situation, and pointed a menacing finger at my dripping shirt.

"*Nicht gut!*" she stated, somewhat shrilly for one so young, I felt. I was informed that the ring on the end of the pull chain was for emergency use only. One was to pull it only when one wished to activate the signal that indicated that one required the services of a chambermaid in order to extricate oneself from the tub. (And inasmuch as neither the chambermaid nor Barbara seemed to feel that I would be requiring such a service, this enchanting safeguard went entirely to waste during the remainder of our brief stay at the Tyrol.)

In fact, Austria, birthplace of my late father and of his father, gave us more than our share of wardrobe problems.

By the time we got to Innsbruck, there were some stubborn spots on a lapel and sleeve of my blue sharkskin suit, and the crease in the trousers seemed to be wandering in all directions. I phoned for valet service and was pleasantly surprised to discover that my call had been relayed to the same lissome chambermaid who had previously come running to rescue me from the tub, and that she bore no grudge over that little misunderstanding.

Would it be possible, I inquired, to have my suit cleaned and returned by suppertime?

"*Ja, ja,*" she declared, with no hesitation.

"Sair goot," I replied, explaining that my wife and I had seats on the 9:16 train to Paris the next morning.

But our chambermaid let us down. When we checked out of the Hotel Tyrol just before nine and kissed the Tedescos good-by, I handed the desk clerk a slip of paper bearing the hastily scrawled words "Van Soutelandelaan 42," Uncle Arthur's address in The Hague, with instructions that my suit should be forwarded to me there, when and if it should find its way back from the cleaners.

Needless to say, I was surprised to be hailed, at precisely 9:16, by an out-of-breath Hotel Tyrol bellhop, just as we were boarding our train.

"One hundred and seventy shillings," he said in flawless English.

"For a single-breasted suit?" I wondered.

"Fifty shillings," the bellhop explained, "was for the taxi to the cleaning factory."

Consulting our conversion chart, we determined that it had cost us exactly $6.63, plus tip, to freshen one everyday suit in Innsbruck, and I was grateful that I had not also entrusted my double-breasted worsted to the mercies of that lissome chambermaid and her partners in crime at the Innsbruck dry-cleaning factory.

Having our dry cleaning delivered to a moving train gave us a certain *éclat* in the eyes of the man who shared our compartment—a chunky native of Graz who carried his papers in a battered briefcase which he clutched to his bosom all the way to Basel—and in that moment we felt very far from home.

"Dear Karen and Gretchen: We are riding on a train in a very pretty country where there still is snow on the mountains. Hope you're having lots of fun with Nana and Grandpop. Love, Mommy and Daddy."

May 20: Grandpop walked Gretchen down to the front gate to meet the mailman, but said he would have to leave Karen behind because she was too heavy. "I am not too heavy," Karen protested, "and that's all there is to it."

Two days in Paris.

Quiche Lorraine at midnight, at a sidewalk café on the Champs Élysées. A knowing wink from the *concierge* at Hotel Vernet. A small, owlish man—a dead ringer for Peter Lorre —furtively peddling what once were considered dirty postcards, at the foot of the stairs to the Sacré Coeur. Cézanne and "Winged Victory" at opposite ends of the Jardin des Tuileries. A bullet-scarred building on rue St. Germain—a hero of France fell here. Lovers everywhere—arm in arm or hand in hand, communicating with their eyes.

And a rendezvous with disaster for my Innsbruck-cleaned suit.

I was wearing that ill-fated suit when Barbara and I allowed our *concierge* to talk us into a Cityrama bus tour, and I tore a gaping hole in the trousers when they caught on the head of an exposed screw on the handle to my seat, after our stop at the Sacred Heart Church.

"Look, mamselle," I said to the mamselle who was in charge of the recorded sight-seeing explanations when she was not hawking bottled *citron* up and down the aisle of our bus. "I must hold your company responsible for this damage." I told her I had paid 170 Austrian shillings merely to have the suit cleaned the day before.

"You will have to see ze manager," I was advised.

In truth, M. Samet, in his manager's office on rue du Vingt-neuf-Juillet, could not have been more gracious. "Give me your trousers, monsieur, and I will take care of everysing."

So we left for The Hague the next morning minus one pair of trousers. And a few short weeks later, the trousers were delivered to Eastleigh, so beautifully rewoven in murky blue that I defy anyone to locate the region where they once were rent.

May 22: Karen seems partial to poetry at bedtime. Pat Farrow phoned today, wondering if we needed anything from the market. Inquisitive Karen: "What's 'wondering'?"

Five days with Uncle Arthur's family in The Hague and environs—and with Mary Kitty, Art's and my stepmother, visiting from California.

The herring fleet heading out to sea, past gray beaches and under gray skies. Girls in blonde pigtails admiring Bobby Seale posters. Flower boxes in barge windows. Fire trucks which will extricate your car from a canal for fifty guilders. Peace activists operating the Anne Frank House. Prostitutes posed in picture windows—difficult to reconcile with the little Dutch girl, wooden shoes, and Hans Brinker. A drive to Gouda for a Sunday morning breakfast of fifteen-inch pancakes. Duchess, the Dutch Breiskys' addlepated boxer, chasing around the garden with her security blanket clutched in her maw. And thoughts turning, ever more frequently, to Karen, Gretchen, and home.

May 26: Mr. and Mrs. Aitkin came to call, to see how Karen was getting along. They said they hadn't seen her since patterning days at Whistling Winds, but Karen remembered them vividly. They were impressed.

Suddenly it was time for good-bys, for packing by dawn's

early light to catch a hop from Amsterdam to London, and on to Bermuda.

Breakfast in Amsterdam. Dinner over the Atlantic. And back in Bermuda in time for lunch.

We got home to Eastleigh ahead of the postcards we had air-mailed from Yugoslavia. John presented Austrian-costumed dolls to his sisters and clomped about the house in his new wooden shoes. And Karen gave us all a word-sign-reading demonstration.

A week later, refreshed and recharged, we were stringing Karen's word signs along the playroom floor to form short sentences. Karen crept slowly from one end of the sentence to the other, reading a word at a time.

"I . . . see . . . my . . . baby . . . and . . . a . . . fish."

CHAPTER XIV

Wondering

The Queen's Birthday—not her real birthday but her "official" birthday—is an occasion for celebration in British Bermuda.

All schools and businesses are closed, and the colony's beaches are as crowded as they ever get. The Bermuda Regiment parades down Front Street in the morning, and in the afternoon bright new frocks and flouncy hats are paraded at the governor's lawn party, to which virtually every Bermuda resident who has taken the pains to sign the Government House guest book is invited.

On our first Queen's Birthday in Bermuda, in June of the previous year, I had taken John and Gretchen, plus Antony and Antonette Francis, down to Hamilton in the morning to see the parading, to hear the bands, and to watch His Excellency the Governor, Lord Martonmere, Privy Councillor and Knight Commander of the Order of St. Michael and St. George, review the troops. The outing was a successful one, except that the twenty-one-gun salute terrified Gretchen, and a can of ginger beer from the cold-drink machine in our office kitchen was required to revive and console her.

Karen had stayed at home and applied her energies to her program on that holiday morning so that she might go to the beach in the afternoon. But if she had missed the Queen's Birthday parade in 1969, she was very much the center of attention on the Queen's Birthday of 1970. She walked a record-breaking twenty steps that day, slowly executed nine somersaults in a row, and crawled along the playroom floor to read a string of words more quickly and more self-confidently than ever:

"I . . . like . . . my . . . cat . . . and . . . pajamas."

Advised that this noteworthy series of achievements would be recorded in one of the notebooks I was keeping on her progress, Karen insisted, "Put down that Mommy takes very good care of us."

"Okay," I said. "But why?"

"Because [foolish question] that will make her happy."

Mommy was, needless to say, happy about the Queen's Birth-day achievements—but she was not happy about a problem that was becoming more and more obvious even as Karen's visual acuity improved: Despite patching, despite all the vision-oriented aspects of her program, she was not using her two eyes together.

"What does Karen see?" remained as great a puzzlement as ever. We were enormously relieved that she was learning to read—large words flashed on a closet wall, then smaller words strung out on the playroom floor—but why did she so often seem to be reading with only one eye? (Either eye, in fact.) And why did she become so confused when we arranged a sentence of strung-out words in two lines rather than one?

You   know   I   like
my   brother   John

Karen was keenly interested when we composed this first two-line sentence one evening, and explained how she should approach it, but she wasn't quite able to put that many words together in the right sequence unless they were in one straight line.

"You . . . know . . . I . . . like . . . John," she read.

"You . . . my . . . brother" was her second try.

And finally her best try: "You . . . know . . . I . . . my . . . brother . . . John."

Once again we would have to seek answers from The In-stitutes in trying to understand how Karen's eyes saw things.

But in the days remaining before our early-July visit to Phila-delphia, we became very much preoccupied with walking.

When left to her own devices, Karen continued to rely on her knees for getting from one place to another, and she would fall to her knees without warning if she felt suddenly insecure while practice-walking. Her walking range continued to increase, however, to the point where it was difficult to get her through the nonwalking parts of her program.

"Karen," we would say, "let's make a deal. If you do three more somersaults, we'll let you walk some more."

On July 5 she took thirty-five steps without falling to her knees, but before we could crow too much about that, the record skyrocketed from thirty-five to sixty.

At some indefinable point she had advanced from being a knee-walker capable of taking a few steps toward outstretched arms, to a little girl who was beginning to think of walking as a means of getting where she wanted to go. She continued to need someone to put her on her feet and to balance her before she was ready to set out, but she learned to change direction with some confidence, and on the evening of July 7 she walked all the way from the bathroom to the kitchen, un-aided, after tooth-brushing time.

"Boy, Karen," I said when I went into her room to say good night, "that was real walking!"

"*Real walking?!*" Karen exclaimed. "Are you sure?"

Whereupon she pushed herself off her bed and insisted on getting in a few minutes' more practice before going to sleep.

"Real walking" proved quite a step for five-year-old Karen, psychologically as well as locomotively. When a photographer friend from New York came to visit us for the first time at Eastleigh, she volunteered to take some candid photo-portraits of the children, and Karen refused to pose sitting down. Walking girls must, it seems, be photographed on their feet.

En route to Philadelphia in mid-July, as Barbara and Karen's plane made its usual stop at Friendship Airport, Karen looked a hundred yards across the tarmac, through a driving rain, recognized "Baltimore" to be a word, rather than some blurred object, and asked what it meant.

The Institutes staff was collectively and enormously pleased at all our new evidence of Karen's reading and walking progress. Karen responded by walking The Institutes' corridors endlessly, if mincingly.

She wasn't, however, nearly ready for school. Because she had reached the age of five, we would have to request permission of Bermuda's school authorities to keep her at home. Sandy Brown suggested that we advance her to smaller flash cards and expose her to new environments and situations outside our home so that she would be more able to adapt to school when (we didn't *say* "if," but we thought it) she was ready to take her place in a classroom. The Institutes staff still couldn't shed much light on when Karen's vision problem might be solved, beyond confirming once again the diagnosis of "alternating divergent strabismus"—but Dr. Thomas did demonstrate anew the fact that the effects of her brain injury continued to affect her entire left side more severely. He covered her two hands and feet, one at a time, and asked Karen to tell him if he was pushing the toes and fingers up or down. Her responses were perfect when he manipulated the digits on her right side, but she had difficulty deciding when he moved her left toes and fingers, guessing wrong almost as often as she guessed correctly. Ladder work—vertical, horizontal, and inclined ladders— was still judged to be the appropriate therapy for helping Karen progress on all fronts.

Karen's knees had become slightly calloused from all her knee-walking and knee-jumping, and a few weeks after the return from Philadelphia her right knee became quite swollen and warm. At the age of five, Karen seemed to be suffering from "housemaid's knee." Our paperback medical encyclopedia suggested that bursitis might be the official diagnosis, and Dr. Bertram Ross, our neighborhood diagnostician, confirmed our findings. Our knee-walking daughter had become a walking girl just in time.

Getting Karen on her feet also proved a boon to Barbara's back. *Thump!*—Karen falling to her knees when she felt insecure while practice-walking—became a more and more familiar sound at Eastleigh, but helping Karen to her feet proved easier for Barbara to take than carrying her.

Karen's progress in the summer of 1970 was due as much as anything to her own get-up-and-go determination, but in addition, an assortment of friends and relatives gave her an assortment of assists. Lee Ann became her first Somerset chum. Two schoolgirls helped carry out the program so Barbara could have some time for her housework and for the rest of the brood during the summer holidays. And nurse Mary Kitty, en route home to San Francisco from Uncle Arthur's in The Hague, counseled the girls on what it means to be a nurse, a career goal Karen had established after her visit to Dr. Ross when she developed housemaid's knee. (Karen didn't aspire to be just *anybody's* nurse; she wished to be Dr. Ross's nurse and had asked him to keep the post open for her.)

Lee Ann Connor was in John's class at school and had come to play with him on that summer's day when she became Karen's friend. But John was up in the tree house with some chums, and the usual "no girls allowed" rule was being enforced—so Lee Ann turned to Karen.

The object of more than her share of adult love and attention for as long as she could remember, Karen didn't seem to mind—perhaps never gave any thought to the fact—that she had never really had a pal her own age. Youngsters such as Brenda Masters, Jamie Descy and Antonette Francis had been friendly and solicitous, but Lee Ann was the first little girl to come any distance especially to play with Karen. Karen was terribly pleased to have acquired this special friend, and of course we saw to it that the welcome mat was always out for Lee Ann; Barbara invariably capitulated when Karen suggested that Lee Ann stay on for supper.

Adela and Susan became Karen's teen friends. Adela Ruberry—guileless and caring, seventeen and sun-loving—had proved such a hit as an occasional baby-sitter that we signed her on to work with Karen on Saturday mornings and whenever she could spare an hour or so after school. And Susan Price—fifteen, firm but gentle, patient, bright and British—became our summer helper. Adela of the bare feet and flower-patched jeans continued to bring cheer and purposeful fancy to Eastleigh on Saturday mornings, and Susan of the rust-red hair did the same on five weekday mornings.

The monotony of the program had become more of a problem and challenge as Karen grew older and more interested in the world outside the playroom. Replacing Barbara with Susan and Adela was in itself a good move toward breaking the monotony for both Barbara and Karen—and working with Karen certainly gave Susan and Adela an opportunity to exercise their imaginations.

Karen had a strong preference for nonsensical sentences when word signs were being strung out on the playroom floor. "That isn't as funny as the one my Daddy made last night, Susan," Karen declared one morning—and Susan made an effort to be more frivolously inventive after that.

Adela, looking back on that silly season, recalls, "I don't think Karen ever said, 'I don't want to do a program'—full stop. She'd say, 'Later,' or 'Wait a minute,' but she never really refused to co-operate. We had a great system of compromising and usually got everything together.

"How could she *possibly* start a program, she would wonder, if I arrived while she was playing with a pile of blocks? Why, if the castle wasn't finished, the dragon would take all the princesses away. And how could I argue?

"One difficult morning I think it was raining. Blah, humid—a blues day. There were at least sixteen kids downstairs, playing tag, climbing, yelling. I was supporting Karen as she moved from rung to rung on her ladder and tried to tell me the color of each bar as we went along. As the chaos from the other kids reached a fine frenzy, Karen couldn't hold onto a bar, and on top of that she said a blue rung was purple.

" 'Oh crumbs, Karen,' I sighed.

"She flaked out in my arms, and in a totally exasperated voice declared, 'Oh, Adela!! How do you expect me to concentrate when those kids are distracting me?'

"Boy, did that faze me. Not only her vocabulary but her conception of the situation. She's a very realistic person as well as having a great streak of imagination."

Also exercising her imagination that summer was my secretary, Vicky, who helped teach Karen the fine art of drinking through a straw. Karen was slightly jealous of John's and Gretchen's ability to sip soft drinks through those long, thin paper tubes. She could pull her drink two thirds of the way up the straw, but no farther.

"Why don't you cut the straw in half?" asked Vicky. We did, and Karen mastered half-straws immediately. Having succeeded at that, she graduated to full-sized straws a week later.

Karen was delighted to be given her first regular chore that summer. The chore was a simple one—carrying the salt and pepper shakers to the table before dinner, and back to the kitchen after dinner—but Karen took it very seriously.

By the end of the summer, Karen, who had seemed word-blind six months earlier, had read her first book—*Play with Us*, Book 1a in the Ladybird Key Words Reading Scheme, first in the stirring adventures of Peter and Jane. She could scarcely scribble, much less write or draw, but with someone holding a reading card to keep her place she was devouring

> Here is Jane
> and here is
> the dog

and asking for more.

John returned to the Sandys Grammar School in mid-September, and Karen and Gretchen were enrolled in a far more exclusive institution of learning. "Our School," they called it, and the two of them comprised the entire student body. All classroom instruction was held in our downstairs playroom-programming room, while extracurricular activities were conducted in the kitchen, on the front porch, and in the garden.

From nine to twelve each weekday morning, the girls didn't know Barbara as "Mommy." She became "Teacher." Barbara had earned her B.S. in art education, but had fled the teaching profession after half a semester of practice-teaching. Her father, a practical man, had had reason to question his wisdom in bankrolling a teacher's certificate for a daughter who proved allergic to children in groups of twenty or more, but "Our School" demonstrated that he had gotten his money's worth.

School was convened each morning with the ringing of a bell—the one on John's bike, which was usually parked in the playroom vestibule. Then, as was the practice at Sandys Grammar, the Lord's Prayer was recited. The program of activities became highly structured, the girls soon insisting that the physical setup be duplicated each day. Karen and Gretchen sat in tiny cane-back chairs made by the blind of Bermuda, and their determinedly proper teacher sat opposite them.

"Teacher" claimed she was given far more attention and respect than Mommy had ever received.

Waking-up exercises were conducted, sometimes in the chairs, sometimes on the floor, sometimes in the form of marching to records. Numbers and letters were taught by rote. Teacher made an alphabet book for each girl; Gretchen demonstrated real ability in the copying and coloring of pictures and words in the book, but Karen could think up words for each letter more quickly.

Ballet lessons were scheduled for two or three mornings a week. Gretchen worked on the "five basic positions," while Karen had to be satisfied with simple plié and relevé warming-up exercises while holding onto the railings on each side of the entrance to the playroom. (Karen really couldn't master the first position, which requires nothing more than bringing your heels together and pointing your toes outward so that your feet form a straight line. She simply couldn't bring her heels together.)

Songs were sung and learned; stories and poems were read and questions asked about them; blocks and beads were used to do simple sums. And toward the end of each hour, when Karen had to take time out for her ladder work, Gretchen was granted "free time" for coloring.

"Sesame Street," sponsored in Bermuda by the Department of Education, proved a useful aide to Barbara in the teaching of numbers. (It was also the first TV program to capture Karen's attention, partly because it didn't confront her with a series of fuzzy, fast-moving images.) As soon as Karen had committed the numbers 1 through 10 to memory, she demonstrated her new skill by dialing my office number for the first time. She informed me excitedly that she had dialed the number by herself, then said abruptly, "Good-by—I'm going to hang you up now!" (The number, fortunately, was an easy one—1-1221. She was unable to manage numbers beyond the "4.")

If the summer of 1970 was the season when Karen conquered the drinking straw, the fall of 1970 was the season when Karen's parents seemed, in retrospect, to have been grasping at straws— those elusive straws that might have held the answer to Karen's problem with vision. We looked first to the world of medical science and later (to my own surprise) to the world of faith healing.

Karen's basic vision problem was that her eyes did not work together. She seemed to be unable to focus quickly on an object, and the problem increased as her distance from the object increased. Since Karen's eyes had never been examined by an ophthalmologist—The Institutes have no eye doctor on their staff—we began to feel, as her focusing problem continued to frustrate us, that another medical opinion might be very useful. It had been a year since Karen had been sent by The Institutes to a Philadelphia optometrist, so perhaps, we felt, a British-trained eye doctor would be able to tell us if her glasses were doing any good and if he could recommend some path that might lead to more meaningful vision.

Barbara took Karen in to Hamilton on a Friday for the initial examination, and I took her in on Saturday morning for the follow-up exam and prognosis.

The doctor's report was both hopeful and distressing. In an effort to hold an object as a single image Karen was, apparently, able to suppress her central vision in either eye—that is, she used only one eye at a time to keep objects in focus. If she were to begin using the same eye consistently, the other eye might become a "lazy eye," and that could mean permanently impaired vision. With surgery—very likely two operations at least—the muscles of Karen's eyes might be slackened to bring the eyes in line, giving her "a much better chance" of correcting her alternating divergence, of focusing her eyes together.

Cosmetically, success would be assured; Karen's eyes would at least *appear* to be working together. The risk itself would be minimal; the procedure, I was told, is a routine one. There would very likely be a need for a second operation, because it is difficult to judge, on the first try, just how much muscle-slackening is required—yet better vision resulting from these operations was not assured. The ophthalmologist would only say that surgery would "improve her chances considerably."

There was no real urgency about having such surgery, we were advised, because Karen seemed to be in no immediate danger of developing a lazy eye. On the other hand, there is a greater chance of success in correcting alternating divergence if the operation is performed before a child is seven.

On the one hand . . .

On the other hand . . .

Is the severing and tying of eye muscles really a "simple procedure"?

In another eighteen months Karen would be seven.

"I'm going to have an eye operation!" Karen said excitedly as we left the doctor's office.

"Maybe," I said, wanting to share her excitement, but not wanting to raise false hopes and not able to minimize Barbara's fear that "no operation is simple."

When I went to Philadelphia with Karen shortly after our session with the ophthalmologist, The Institutes did indeed veto eye surgery. For the first time, the IAHP directors and a well-regarded medical specialist were at odds on the best care for Karen, so Art Sandler took great pains to explain his opposition.

His reasoning was rooted in the most basic of IAHP theories—that Karen's visual problem was a brain problem, not an eye problem, and that if a surgeon began tampering with her eye muscles, her vision might actually be adversely affected. Her eyes would continue to receive the same signals from her brain, so that in time they might be pulled back to where they had been before the operation—with weakened eye muscles as the end result. Art Sandler said The Institutes staff had never seen a brain-injured youngster whose visual acuity had been permanently improved as a result of such an operation.

We were instructed to stimulate Karen's eyes alternately with a four-cell flashlight, in order to make her eye muscles work maximally and to make the crystalline lens—which focuses the light on the retina—more flexible. Somersaulting and rolling herself over and over were other ways we could make her eye muscles work maximally. "Brachiation" was yet another technique—swinging forward on an overhead ladder like a monkey, with Barbara or myself kneeling behind her, hands on her hips, letting her do as much as she could for herself. (Apes, we were reminded more than once, are unsurpassed in hand-eye coordination.)

Eye-patch glasses were recommended—one pair with a black opaque lens on the right and with no lens on the left side, the other with a black lens on the left. The patches we previously used had blocked her vision in one eye altogether; these eye-patch glasses would block the central vision, but not the peripheral vision. They were meant to help assure—without limiting her field of vision—that Karen did not develop a lazy eye.

Finally, we were to try stimulating her peripheral vision by gluing a piece of black paper the size of a quarter inside a flashlight lens, then flashing the light at a range of three inches in order to surround the retina with light.

But Karen didn't see what this exercise should have caused her to see. Neither was she exercising her eye muscles as intended by swinging from rung to rung on her overhead ladder "with little or no assistance." She didn't have nearly enough strength in her left hand to perform such a feat, and the goal given us by The Institutes seemed unrealistic.

In truth, the conflict between ophthalmology and The Institutes had left us uneasy, and while we accepted the antisurgery opinion, we didn't feel really confident in our new visual program.

Seeking the advice of a Bermudian eye doctor had been a kind of grasping at straws—a display of less than total faith in The Institutes. And when a farming couple from Somerset, England—Gerald and Agnes Hooper—came to Bermuda in early November, we were psychologically prepared for another kind of reaching out.

"Our Lord instructed his disciples to preach the gospel and to heal the sick," the rector of St. James Church, Somerset, told us one Sunday, "and the church seems to have forgotten that second instruction over the years." Then he introduced the Hoopers who, he said, had been given the gift of healing and had demonstrated on many occasions what faith and a laying-on-of-hands can achieve.

St. James Church was crowded on the night the Hoopers first explained their healing mission. Barbara went to the service while I baby-sat, but as the coffee-hour discussion was about to get under way in the church hall she slipped out a side door and came home. She couldn't take any more—wanting desperately to believe that Karen could be healed by a laying-on-of-hands, but feeling intense pain in the act of hoping. She asked me to sit in on the discussion hour.

I went to the church hall that evening, and later we took Karen to two healing services in the church, during one of which the Anglican Bishop of Bermuda himself, in his long purple cassock, stepped forward to be healed.

Later in the week we took Karen to the rectory for a private healing session. It was a special evening for Karen. She was dressed in the new granny gown Barbara had made for her and was going to stay up beyond her normal bedtime. "I'm going to be healed!" she said proudly to her brother and sister as we left, not really knowing what to expect, but certainly not expecting any sudden transformation.

The Hoopers said they were certain that their healing mission could help Karen, gradually, and urged us to continue with "absent healing," praying briefly at 4 P.M. (9 P.M. British time) daily, in company with them and with their healing groups in Britain and elsewhere.

Over the previous three and a half years, we felt we had seen Karen healed by a kind of faith—by the hands and skills and prayers of people who had faith that a child can overcome the loss of millions of brain cells. This healing process had been gradual, and we had no reason to believe it would stop.

We couldn't help but be impressed by the Hoopers' sincerity and lack of pretension, and by their belief that God had seen fit to heal others through their hands. Yet as I considered this healing mission which had come virtually to our doorstep, and in which we had (with some skepticism on my part) participated, I found myself of two spirits—wishing an instant miracle for Karen while not really wanting to believe that this series of services should make a difference. Surely, I thought, a God does not listen more attentively to those who raise their prayers in unison, at 4 P.M. Bermuda time. Surely He would not determine a child's future on the basis of whether or not the child's parents chanced to live in a parish that happened to be visited by someone with a gift of healing. Surely a child's destiny would not be shaped irrevocably by his or her parents' degree of faith. Surely a God who loves all His children would not demand participation in any ceremonial laying-on-of-hands, prior to dispensing His miracles.

While the Hoopers of Somerset, England, were carrying out their mission in Somerset, Bermuda, I began, by chance, to read Peter Nichols's play, *Joe Egg*. The play had opened on Broadway on February 1, 1968, and the New York *Times* had carried both a review and an interview with the playwright. The "Joe Egg" of the title, the review had stated, was a ten-year-old child named Josephine, brain-damaged since birth, spastic, subject to fits, unable to move, to see, to talk, declared by medical science to be "a vegetable." Joe's father had accepted her condition, but in order to live with it had to affect a kind of outrageous, corrosive humor. Nothing is unbearable if you can find a means of laughing at it, he had seemed to say.

Because my thoughts at that point in life were rather consumed with Karen and with my long-shot try at playwriting, I read and reread the *Times* review of the play, and especially Vincent Canby's interview with the man who wrote it. Peter Nichols was said to be a forty-year-old English schoolmaster turned actor-writer—and the father of four children, including a brain-damaged daughter.

"To that extent," playwright Nichols told reporter Canby, "the play is autobiographical. We used to make up fantasies about the child. But we are not the parents in the play. We put our child in a home, which, of course, is what the parents in the play should have done."

Somewhat awed by this writer who was able to bare such an intensely personal and difficult decision, finding humor in despair—and wanting to share the answers we were beginning to find for Karen—I had sat down at my typewriter in February 1968 and addressed a letter to Peter Nichols in care of the Brooks Atkinson Theater in New York. I told him that our family situation almost duplicated his—except that we had been directed to a place called The Institutes for the Achievement of Human Potential, and so had been able to reject a doctor's advice that Karen be placed in a home. I invited him and his wife to phone us, and perhaps come to Connecticut to see Karen and talk about The Institutes at some time during the month or six weeks the *Times* said he intended to spend in New York.

He replied six months later, from his home in England:

Dear Mr. Breisky,

. . . If you ever saw the play, you will have gathered what an extreme case I took. It was our daughter's, of course, and I think it's pretty safe to say that she survived a birth that should have delivered her stillborn. It was one of those misfortunes of human ingenuity that she lived at all. She has never really shown any sign of intelligence, perception or awareness, beyond the reaching out described in the play, a few smiles and a blinking of the eyes in strong light. Your own girl's illness was, of course, a far sadder matter, as by the time she suffered it you must have grown used to her as a person. I refer to that, too, in the play when the mother says there are far worse cases than hers and imagines that Joe might have become a real person before the disaster happened. It is wonderful to hear how much you have done for Karen and, had our stay in America been a shade less fraught, I might have managed to arrange a meeting. I was ill and the intense cold of your winter finally sent us scampering to the airliner. Also we had our three young children with us—a great mistake, I think, but what else could we do with them?

Of course we did all we could in the first months of our discovery that Abigail wasn't normal. We tried the best children's hospital in the country, a Harley Street pediatrician, his teacher and a school with a high reputation near the town where we lived in Devon. We too followed a rigorous course of exercises, but the great problem in Abigail's case is that she is acutely epileptic and any excitement of the brain, such as achieving success in a new task, brings on a sequence of fits which have to be sedated. The sedation makes her so sleepy that she can no longer pay any attention. How you break that circle of conditions is something nobody seems to know.

Life is earnest and real. Abigail is in permanent care in a mental hospital, along with a ward full of other patients in similar conditions. We have three other children, all under five, and they're a full-time job. I am not a particularly optimistic man and would be more interested in preventing accidents of this kind than in giving up my life to cure them. I think that most of the cases I've known have been very serious ones, where a great deal of optimism would be needed to discern any hope at all.

Anyway, thank you for writing and comparing our situations. I hope Karen continues to improve and best wishes with your writing.

Yours sincerely,
Peter Nichols

We didn't go to New York to see *Joe Egg*, but I ordered a copy of the play when I saw an ad for a paperback edition. That copy sat on or near my night table for two years, unopened. I got only as far as the back-cover comments of a London *Observer* reviewer—"a remarkable play about a nightmare all women must have dreamed at some time, and most men: living with a child born so hopelessly crippled as to be, as the father in it says brutally, 'a human parsnip.' For all that, it has to be described as a comedy, one of the funniest and most touching I've seen . . ." Neither Barbara nor I wanted to read further. Weren't prepared to, somehow.

But in November 1970, more than two years after Peter Nichols had answered my letter, and while Gerald and Agnes Hooper were in the midst of their healing mission in Bermuda, I reached for *Joe Egg* one night.

Toward the end of Act One, Brian ("Bri") and Sheila commence a series of ritual playlets wherein they relive, in a grossly exaggerated way, some of the experiences they had gone through, or at least contemplated going through, with Joe.

In dialogues they hold alternately with each other and the audience, Sheila plays herself while Brian takes on other roles. For a while he is a pediatrician with a music-hall German accent, telling Sheila that Joe's period of observation is over and that it is high time she be released from the hospital.

Bri: Vell, mattam, zis baby off yours has now been soroughly tested and ve need ze bets razzer badly so it's better you take her home. I sink I can promise she von't be any trouble. Keep her vell sedated you'll hartly know she's zere.

Sheila wants to know the results of all the tests. She yearns to know what her daughter can *do*.

Bri: Do? She can't do nozzing at all.

Sheila can't accept that. She demands an explanation. Bri, as the doctor, tells her to imagine a switchboard with all the lines buzzing and flashing until the stress becomes too great and Joe has an epileptic fit.

Sheila: Isn't there *any*thing at all we can do?
Bri: But jawohl! You must feed her, vosh her nappies, keep her varm. Just like any ozzer mozzer.
Sheila: But for how long?
Bri: Who can tell? Anysing can happen, you know zat. Diphtheria, pneumonia . . . vooping cough . . . Colorado beetle.

They come out of character for a while; then Bri becomes a vicar who reassures Sheila that Joe is not God's way of punishing her for her premarital affairs.

Bri: My dear, your child's sickness doesn't please God. In fact, it completely brings Him down.
Sheila: Why does He allow it then?
Bri: How can we know?

Sheila tells the vicar she doesn't want explanations. She has asked the people who should have been able to explain, and they couldn't.

Bri: What *do* you want?
Sheila: Magic.
Bri: I was slowly coming round to that. Once or twice, over the years, we have had in this parish children like your daughter.
Sheila: Just as bad?
Bri: Oh, yes, I'm sure, quite as bad. Now for those poor innocents I did the Laying On Of Hands bit.
Sheila: What is that?
Bri: A simple ceremony in your own home. A few prayers, a hymn or two, a blessing, an imposition of hands. Nothing flashy.

Sheila probes for details. Did he have any luck with the other children?

> *Bri:* There was one boy—no better than Joe—made such rapid recovery after I'd done the Laying On a few times—the medicos confessed themselves bewildered. He's twelve now and this spring he was runner-up in the South West Area Tap-Dancing Championships.
>
> *Sheila:* How fantastic!

They break out of the sketch, and as Bri drops his vicar imitation, Sheila rebukes him, for what must be the nth time, because he had, indeed, refused a vicar's offer of a laying-on-of-hands for Joe.

> *Sheila:* He was a good man, kind and sincere.
>
> *Bri:* He was, yes.
>
> *Sheila:* And that boy was cured.
>
> *Bri:* Certainly improved. And, yes, he was the runner-up in the South West Area Tap-Dancing Championships. *But.* He never *had* been as bad as Joe.
>
> *Sheila:* I don't care—
>
> *Bri:* I looked into it—
>
> *Sheila:* You shouldn't have.
>
> *Bri:* I spoke to people—
>
> *Sheila:* Where's the harm? What else did we have?
>
> *Bri:* Nothing.
>
> *Sheila:* Well!
>
> *Bri:* I'd rather have nothing than a lot of lies.
>
> *Sheila:* You're unusual.
>
> *Bri:* First he'd have done it for us, then he'd have got a few of his mates in to give the prayers more Whoosh! More Pow! And before long he'd have had us doing it in church gloated over by all those death-watch beetles like the victims of a disaster.
>
> *Sheila:* It could have worked. He might have magicked her.
>
> *Bri:* I'm sure it was best to stop it then than later on—after he'd raised your hopes. Sheila—(*She looks at him, smiles.*)
>
> Anyway. If the vicar had got her going, she'd only have had one personality. As it is, we've given her dozens down the years.

Sheila (to audience): As soon as we were admitted to the freema-
sonry of spastic parents, we saw she had even less character
than the other children. So we began to make them for her.

They recall some of the characters of their invention, and as
the act is drawing to a close, Sheila tells the audience: "I join
in these jokes to please him. If it helps him live with her, I
can't see the harm, can you? He hasn't any faith she's ever going
to improve. Where I have, you see. . . ."

And so Sheila, a character who clung to hope despite the
reality of seizures, and yet had been created by "a not particularly
optimistic man," reminded me that we were but two parents
among millions who over the years have had faith and yet have
doubted . . . and that life goes on.

Life, and the healing process, went on well for Karen. On
November 14, with two adult hands barely touching the small
of her back, more to assure her than to balance her, she climbed
the two small steps from the playroom to the downstairs guest
room. She had to be coaxed into taking the first step, hesitantly
and uncertainly; then confidently, squealing with delight, she
conquered the final step and trotted across the room, arguing
not at all when she was declared "a climbing girl" rather than
a mere walking girl.

On the way home from Sunday school the next morning she
and Gretchen sang, "I am *h-a-p-p-y* . . . I am *h-a-p-p-y* . . . I
know I am—I'm sure I am . . . *h-a-p-p-y*." But by that evening, when she was to have gone to St. James for the last of the
healing services, Karen had all the symptoms—fever, headache,
and spotty throat—of a virus from which Gretchen had just recovered, so we put her to bed. I recorded in a notebook the ironic
fact that Karen seemed "too sick to be healed."

For all her problems and frustrations, Karen *was* h-a-p-p-y. We
never doubted that. We'll never know how much of her good
disposition is a by-product of all the affection that has been lavished on her by the Dolly Beans, the Arian Francises, and the
Ronnies and Alastairs in her life, and how much is innate good

nature. In any case her demonstrativeness seemed boundless. "I love my Mommy," became a daily litany. "I want to hug you . . . You're the best Mommy in the world." Visitors likewise were apt to get the big-hug treatment. Living in a tactile world for so long, Karen had been picked up, held, squeezed, and programmed daily, had been told endlessly that she was "doing great work"—so she had to be excused for failing to be wary of strangers, for imagining that the world is filled with nice people.

Wondering . . .

We wondered about her vision. We wondered when and if she would be able to graduate from Barbara's school to John's. And we wondered if her boundless affection wasn't setting her up for a jolt of disillusionment once she entered a school outside her home.

We would continue to wonder about these things in coming months—but it was questioning-wonder touched frequently with amazement-wonder as Karen's progress demonstrated a quickening of her desire for independence.

In mid-December, an impressive week of achievements for Righty: He turned on a bathroom faucet, turned a doorknob and pushed open a door, and removed both of Karen's shoes.

"I'm getting tired of baby-sitters," John declared one evening as Barbara and I were dressing for an evening out and I announced that I would go pick up our buoyant Bermudian sitter, Miss Roberts. "I'm too big for them."

"And I'm too little for baby-sitters," Gretchen chimed in.

Karen, of course, had become "too medium for them."

At about that same time, Karen asked me to record the fact that her favorite doll, Baby Elizabeth, had gone to the hospital.

"Why?" I wondered.

"To have her independence taken out."

Nana and Grandpop came for Christmas, and Nana was given the challenge of trying to give Karen an important nudge toward school readiness—a lesson in letter-making. While Karen's reading level had advanced to Book 4 in the Ladybird series, her writing hadn't gone beyond a scribble, and usually a faint scribble at that. Her Righty had learned to grasp a pencil or crayon with increasing confidence, but after months of occasional effort with Adela and Susan, and with Barbara in "Our School," she still hadn't mastered anything as disciplined as a circle.

Chalk and slate, we had learned, were considerably easier to work with than pencil and paper. A heavy white chalk line on a black slate is easy to make, easy to erase, and easy to read. A week of chalk work with her grandmother seemed to be just what Karen needed. By week's end she had conquered x and o, and declared herself ready to try f—"so we can make 'fox.'" Her x's didn't always cross where they should; the o's sometimes resembled c's lying on their backs; her letters varied greatly in size and they trooped up hills and down into valleys when they should have been marching in a straight line. But they were her first recognizable written symbols, and she was on her way.

Grandpop, meanwhile, tested Karen's ability to think up sentences using her flash-card word signs, and was amazed at the results.

"Make a sentence with this word, Karen."

Karen read the word thoughtfully. "'Sweet' . . . 'Gretchen likes sweet candy.' . . . Wait a minute! Let me make a better one: 'Karen and Gretchen would like to have a sweet for to-night's dessert.'"

"Let's try two words this time."

"'Red' and 'we.'" Five-second pause. Then, "I've got a good one! 'John says we want a red soccer ball for Christmas.'"

Karen the storytelling champion was declared Karen the sentence-making champion.

My goal of the moment with Karen, to be practiced during our "evening program" ritual, was an unglamorous one: Stooping.

Stooping means bending your body forward and downward without collapsing into a heap or falling face first into whatever you are bending over to do.

Stooping is not easy when you still feel more sure of yourself on your knees than on your feet and are falling and tripping frequently; so our first goal was simply to bend over far enough to touch the roof of a dollhouse or the seat of a play-table chair. Before long, however, Karen had graduated to picking up a four-battery lantern by its handle.

The student body in "Our School" was reduced from two to one that winter as Gretchen, at four, reached the age when she could be enrolled in a government nursery school.

"When can *I* go to school?" Karen wanted to know.

"Maybe not too long from now" was all Barbara dared promise.

Meanwhile, during a lesson in "Our School" on the numbers 1 through 12:

Teacher: "It's ten o'clock now, Karen. In one hour, what time will it be?"

Karen: "Time for 'Sesame Street'?"

In late January, a new program from The Institutes, loaded with ladder work: more overhead ladder drill, plus a vertical ladder for climbing and another ladder to be ascended at a forty-five-degree angle, to put more weight on her left hand—all aimed at improving vision, Lefty, balance, and chest expansion.

At The Institutes a six-year-old youngster named Lisa, confined to a wheelchair and impressed with Karen's progress since the last time they had seen one another, declared grandly, "It pleases me to see you walking so well."

By early March, capital *K* and capital *F* had been added to the inventory of letters Karen could write, and she was working on *N* and *P*. She could count by ones to thirty, by fives to twenty-five, and by tens to a hundred. As a reward for these academic feats, she was granted a long-cherished wish—a ride on the back of my motorbike. She clung to me for dear life, and a too-large safety helmet kept slipping down so that her eyes were virtually covered for most of that brief ride, but that didn't diminish the excitement.

Wednesday, March 24, 1971: Karen blew her nose for the first time. She didn't hold the handkerchief in place; her achievement lay in getting her brain to command her lungs, lips and diaphragm to work pretty much in concert so that she could expel air from her lungs through her nose with sufficient gusto.

One April evening, "Uncle Siegfried" came to call. This guttural-voiced grouch, a dead ringer for Karen's father, appeared in the playroom during one of our after-dinner program sessions, noted that Karen was not putting forth maximum effort, and shouted, "Get to vurk, you lazy bummer, and schtop all zis fooling aroundt!"

Karen responded by ascending her vertical ladder in record time, and thus Uncle Siegfried took his place alongside Geraldine in our family's folklore. The evening programs had become something of a bore, so that even an ogre such as Siegfried was welcomed by Karen. (To assure that this Teutonic tyrant himself didn't become a bore, I created a family of program-time uncles, all shameless stereotypes: "Uncle-a-Tony," who consumed great quantities of spaghetti and meat-a-balls for breakfast, lunch and dinner; "Uncle Friday," a drawling, slow-moving southerner who slept his life away, appearing every Saturday morning for programming, after having promised to come on Friday; "Uncle Tob," whose real name was Tom but who was suffering from an

incurable cold-id-the-doze; "Uncle Louie," a whining sort, suffering from an inferiority complex and convinced that Karen was
the only human being in the world who cared what happened to
him; and "Uncle Sunday," who looked, behaved and sounded
like the father of John, Karen and Gretchen, and could be recognized by no one but Karen.)

On her fifth birthday, Karen had demonstrated her newfound
walking skill with a quick succession of tottery steps and then—
crash! into someone's arms. On birthday number six—April 27,
1971—she walked across the living room, then bent over to pick
up, without losing her balance, Ladybird Book 6a, which she
had just completed. She was able to read many of the words on
her birthday cards and wore a fashionable new pantsuit as she
played hostess to a party for her new friend Lee Ann, plus
Antony and Antonette, Miss Roberts, Adela and Susan, and a
couple of friends from Sunday school—the rector's daughter and
the undertaker's son.

Early May: a visit to Friendship Vale, Bermuda's school for
handicapped children. "Special education," Bermuda-style. Deaf
children in one wing, children with hurt brains—severely hurt
in most cases—in the other. Patient, concerned teachers and
generally happy, loving children. But getting there would mean
a bus ride for Karen of almost an hour and a half each way,
each day. There was a physical therapist on the staff, but she
wouldn't have time for much of Karen's program. The teacher-
pupil ratio was good, but certainly didn't approach the one-to-
one ratio at home. And there seemed so little challenge: Youngsters who were wheelchair-bound, mostly listless and with poor
head control, seemingly very much in need of stimulation.
Friendship Vale was not for Karen.

Mid-May: another visit to Philadelphia. Karen's chronological
age was seventy-three months, and her neurological age com-
puted at forty-two months. Mobility, vision, and manual compe-

tence continued to hold this figure down, we were told, and a modified program of ladder work was prescribed once again. Now, however, Karen was also to be hung upside down for five minutes at a time, suspended by straps of belting around her ankles. Good for chest expansion and to make her flex her eye muscles. We were to play eye games while she was upside down, and to hang her from a single hook, twisting her a couple of turns, then releasing her and letting her spin.

The Institutes' Art Sandler agreed that Friendship Vale was not for Karen—and also agreed, when Karen was out of earshot, that we might try enrolling her in Sandys Grammar in the fall, on a trial basis, mornings only, so that she could continue her program work in the afternoons. The IAHP was greatly impressed with her reading and writing progress and was optimistic about giving school a try.

First step in the procedure for enrolling Karen in Sandys Grammar was to "interview" the head teacher.

"*You* go," said Barbara, who found it difficult to face the possibility that Karen might be turned down. "Please."

Mrs. Elford and I discussed Karen's problems and potential in detail, and her reaction was hopeful. But the idea of half-day school could be a problem. Regulations, you know. Mrs. Elford would have to write to the Department of Education for a ruling. In the meantime, I was advised, we had better not build up Karen's hopes too much.

Empire Day 1971: The tooth fairy calls at Eastleigh and leaves a twenty-five-cent reward for Karen's first tooth. What's more, Karen *sees* the tooth fairy. Pressed for a description, our daughter declares, "She had brown skin and a little blue dress and red shoes."

Memorial Day 1971: Scott Lewis, a new and well-freckled kid in the neighborhood—John's age and part of a Canadian navy family from Halifax—is playing in John's room. Scott and John come down the stairs to the playroom two at a time, but when Scott enters the room and sees Karen suspended by her feet and being spun like a top, he stops short and draws in his breath.

"Mr. Breisky," he says—and there is respect in his voice—"is that a punishment?"

This has, indeed, been a year for wondering.

CHAPTER XV

"Real School"

Psychologically and academically, Karen Luise Breisky must have been as ready for school as any youngster entering an Infant One class in Bermuda in the fall of 1971.

Karen was "up." She had done well in Barbara's one-room school, and Susan Price had been signed on for the summer again, to help with school readiness work as well as to plug away at the IAHP program and to help organize late-morning expeditions to the beach.

By midsummer she was able to produce a reasonable facsimile of *K-a-r-e-n* on her slate, and Susan and Barbara were able to recognize eyes, nose, mouth, ears and hair in drawings that had previously seemed mere scribbles to everyone but Karen herself.

As summer drew to a close, we learned that Karen's acceptance as a mornings-only student would take place more or less by default. Mrs. Elford, the headmistress, told us she had had no response from the Department of Education to her written request concerning Karen, so why didn't we just give it a try.

"Real school," Karen said when we made it official. "Oh boy."

The name of this "real school" had been changed over the summer from Sandys Grammar to Somerset Primary. In order to further the process of racial integration, a smaller, virtually all-black school was to be "amalgamated" with Sandys Grammar over a three-year period.

The Somerset Primary uniforms Barbara made for Karen and Gretchen appealed greatly to both of them. Individualists they might be, but when it came to getting together a school wardrobe, both had a desire to "be the same."

Gretch, almost two months short of her fifth birthday, was just barely old enough to be accepted in Infant One with Karen. Barbara and Mrs. Elford agreed, however, that it would be a good idea to put the girls in different classrooms—so each could develop her own friends and so Gretchen wouldn't be called upon regularly to come to her sister's aid.

We hoped very hard that Karen was prepared to compete in "real school." Her word-recognition work was fine, but she needed someone to help keep her place when she was reading. Her writing was labored and often incomprehensible—but writing isn't that important in the first year of school. She was a great listener—and that certainly was in her favor. But what of all the small skills schoolchildren were assumed able to perform with their hands and legs and eyes—cutting, pasting, buttoning, hide-and-go-seeking, pulling a chair up to a work table? Could she manage? Would her teacher be able to give her special attention? (Should she *have* special attention?)

And what of the inevitable wondering looks and questions? The Institutes staff had agreed she should not wear her eye patch to school—she would appear "different" enough without it—but even so, was she prepared to handle all the challenges she would face? Should Barbara have a chat with her teacher ahead of opening day, so that the teacher might think about how to explain Karen's special needs (and heroic achievements) to the rest of the class?

These were problems that existed in *our* minds, not Karen's, and like so many of life's anticipated problems, most of them evaporated—while we were to be confronted with a few problems we had not anticipated.

Soon the first day of school was upon us. Gretchen was assigned to Mrs. Hill's class, where she met many of her chums from nursery school. Karen, assigned to the class of Miss Gillian Edney, of Oxford, England, finished her first half-day of school at 11:45, very tired, and took a nap—but by the time I returned home from work that evening she was bubbling over with news of the great event:

"Tracy cried and cried, but she got over it. . . . I know some musical insterments—the banjo, the guitar, the violin, the drum. We're all learning some new songs. And I know arithmetic! . . . All the kids are new, Daddy, including me."

Miss Edney reported to Barbara, "The morning went quite well. Karen really seems quite independent."

Wisely, Miss Edney had not made any special fuss over Karen, nor had she said anything about her to the class. To most of the children, Karen was looked upon at first as a little girl with a walking problem—"crippled," a couple of them said. Karen was given a seat at the table nearest Miss Edney, who had decided the best policy was simply "to quietly be there when she needed help."

After the first day, there was no shortage of little girls willing to lend Karen a hand. The ten- and eleven-year-olds almost smothered her with help at times, so much so that Gretchen developed some short-lived complexes about the school. The minute Barbara would drive into the school yard in the mornings, a band of girls, usually including Lee Ann Connor, would rush to the car, look straight through Gretchen (who, after all, didn't need any help), and ask if they could escort Karen to Miss Edney's room.

"School is getting better and better," Karen reported before completing her first week of half-days. "I went outside at recess today."

Just as the best gifts often come in small packages, so may the most meaningful acts of friendship often come in small gestures. In Karen's case such a gesture came from an impish, wide-eyed five-year-old French-Canadian classmate named Lyne Genereux, who sat at Karen's table and who somehow knew intuitively that what Karen wanted more than anything—although she had never said as much—was simply to be treated like the other kids.

Lyne's gesture—the one that sealed her friendship with Karen —came just two weeks after the school year had started. The girls in the class were getting dressed for "PT" (physical training), and Karen was sitting on the sidelines as the other youngsters slipped off their dresses.

Lyne needed a hand to unzip her dress, and she solicited help from the pair of hands least able to perform the task efficiently.

"Karen," she said, "will you pull down my zipper for me?"

Karen was enormously pleased, and she related the story for me in detail when I got home that evening. "She had to stand very still," Karen reported, "but I got it!"

Thank you, Lyne Genereux.

Karen Breisky, Lyne Genereux, and a steadfast, sentimental little citizen named Sharon Bailey became the best of pals. They would give the stampeding hordes a chance to clear the corridor at recess time before heading out to the playground, to assure that Karen didn't get trampled, and on most days they devised activities in which Karen could take part.

One day Karen was caught in the mad rush and knocked down. She was terrified, Miss Edney reported, and it took a few minutes to calm her down—but we thought it significant that the incident was reported to us by Miss Edney and not by Karen.

"What do you like best about school?" I asked at dinner one evening.

"Miss Edney" was Karen's reply. "And making things. And I have lots of friends."

"And what *don't* you like about school?"

Karen could think of no answer to that question.

The boys in Karen's class weren't, as a group, as considerate as the girls. To some, she was at first an unknown quantity, and they kept their distance. One persisted in giving her fish-eyed stares, and one mimicked her a couple of times.

Somehow her limited, slightly fuzzy range of vision made Karen unaware of those few staring and mimicking incidents— and before long the boys were won over.

She asked the boy with the fish-eye stare to help her with the clasp on her lunch box (which she toted to school for "little lunch"—midmorning snack), and after that he was volunteering his help almost every day.

"Men!" said Barbara.

One of the boys pushed her to the floor on a couple of occasions—but many of the other girls in the class had been given doses of the same pushing-around treatment by the boys, so Karen was as much flattered, or puzzled, as offended.

"Why, Mommy?" she asked. "Why did he push me down?"

Perhaps being pushed down and knocked down was just the inspiration Karen needed in order to master the set of skills required to get herself up off the floor and into a standing position without a helping hand. In mid-October we told Karen about some friends from Pittsburgh who were coming for Christmas, and asked if she thought she would be able to stand herself up by that time. Then I promised that when she achieved this goal, I would write the news in her notebook in extra-big letters. So, without further ado, she stood up then and there, and I inscribed the words—

KAREN STOOD
HERSELF UP TODAY
WITHOUT LEANING
ON ANYTHING!!

"The other children came running to tell me about it," Miss Edney reported, when Karen repeated the standing-up feat in school the next day.

Karen must have been a bit of an enigma even to her friends in Infant One. She was a little girl who had trouble staying on her feet, and couldn't catch a ball. A little girl whose writing was illegible to most people and whose eyes didn't tell her how rude a few of the little boys were and who had trouble finding her place in her reader. Yet a little girl who was the most advanced reader in the class and who expressed herself very well (always volunteering when it came time to report "news," Miss Edney told us) and was eager to *try* anything.

Her first report card was a beautiful document:

Reading: "Book 5. Karen reads well."

Speech: "Good. Karen must not be shy about taking part in class discussion."

Creative Writing: "Karen has a good imagination. She describes things; I write them and she copies underneath."

Handwriting: "Karen is working very hard with her writing. There has been a definite improvement."

Numbers: "Karen's oral work with numbers is good."

Teacher's Comments: "Karen perseveres with all her work. She has a very good relationship with the other children and takes part in all class activities. A very pleasant member of the class."

Head Teacher's Comment: "Well done, Karen!"

A member of the class—that was the comment we prized above all.

"Real school" was going so well by mid-December that The Institutes staff agreed we should let Karen return to school three afternoons a week, provided she squeezed in six programs on those days when she returned to school, and eight on other days.

The idea of returning to school had been Karen's. "Mommy," she had asked more than once, "couldn't I go back today if I eat my lunch fast and do a couple of programs?"

Barbara's after-school work with Karen continued to emphasize hand-eye exercises, and resulted, we were satisfied, in slowly but steadily increasing control of her hands. She began, laboriously, making pictures that were reasonable facsimiles of the sun, a house, a stick figure, and a tree.

Barbara bought the girls their own set of mixing bowls, bake pans, and cake mixes, and on rainy afternoons Karen began to achieve, through practice, an ability to stir, measure, and pour. Although the technique of folding paper napkins continued to elude her, she managed to sort the napkins and silver with increasing skill and by the end of the year was doing most of the table-setting herself, even to the point of carrying (while we held our breath) saucers and half-filled drinking cups from kitchen to dining room.

A further round of IAHP-prescribed techniques aimed at improving her field of vision or her focusing ability proved as disappointing and frustrating as previous efforts, however—or at least it was as difficult as ever to measure any immediate results.

Binoculars were suggested by The Institutes as a means of extending her distance vision, as an exercise in telling her eyes what they should be seeing out there beyond where she was accustomed to looking. But we had no success with them at all, perhaps because binoculars must be adjusted and focused by each individual user, and Karen was unable to tell us when they were focused properly for her.

Three months after the binoculars experiment we were told to order a "3-D Fusion Game" set from the Keystone View Company—3-D red-and-green filter glasses, a small wooden pointer and a series of 3-D picture cards. This "game" was designed to help kids with a fusion problem to straighten their eyes and develop good teamwork between them. Objective No. 1 was to help them translate images received by the two eyes into a single mental impression; the second objective was to make them able to judge the relative distances of objects. But this home-training project proved as much of a flop as the binoculars. Karen enjoyed the game reasonably well, but couldn't get consistently correct answers even to the first lesson.

Still, her close-up vision seemed to be improving, and that translated itself into better schoolwork. One day as Barbara drove into the school yard a pretty, blue-eyed classmate of Karen's came running over to the car and announced breathlessly, "Today we made *R*'s, Mrs. Breisky, and Miss Edney said Karen made very good ones." By Christmastime Karen remained the most advanced book-reader in her class—a record she cherished enormously.

On one of the very few occasions when Karen was deliberately cut out by any of the girl members of the class, Karen responded by using her reading skill as a weapon—and thereby demonstrated that she was learning how to defend herself in a give-and-take situation. The incident took place at the toy playhouse in the school, where a posted sign declared, "Three may play." Karen saw a twosome heading for the playhouse and decided to be number three, but the doorway was barred to her when she arrived.

At first Karen didn't know how to react, so (as she related the story that evening), "I just stood there." But finally she remembered the "Three may play" sign on the playhouse, and in a rare display of spitefulness declared, *"You* can't read!"—which happened to be true.

(Women!)

Lee Ann Connor was the first Somerset girl to invite Karen to a "big girl's party." The occasion was Lee Ann's eighth birthday. Karen came home with three prizes, and promptly sat me down on our living room love seat to assure that I recorded the achievement properly.

"Put down that I won one ring, one bracelet, and a game of pick-up sticks. I got them for throwing balls in a bucket and for bingo."

"Got it," I responded.

"And remember that 'Lee Ann' starts with an *L*."

For her own seventh birthday, Karen invited Lee Ann, Sharon, Lyne and five other youngsters from the class and neighborhood, and joined happily in the games Barbara had organized—a peanut hunt (very difficult for Karen) and musical chairs (relatively easy, for she had had considerable sitting-down-in-a-hurry experience).

Baby-sitter Adela Ruberry brought Karen, without consulting her parents, a pair of guinea pigs, sex undetermined, whom Karen named Ernie and Bert, after the "Sesame Street" characters. These were declared by Karen to be "the greatest present ever."

Because Karen, at a recent visit to The Institutes, had declared that "cutting" and "riding a bike" were the two things she would like most to be able to do, Barbara and I made the rounds of Bermuda's bike shops and came home with a Karen-sized two-wheeler with training wheels.

No one at The Institutes had suggested that we go out and buy Karen a bicycle, but we had always been encouraged to help

Karen reach out for difficult goals. So we began by putting her on her back a couple of times a day and moving her legs in a simulated bicycle-pedaling exercise. Then we sat her on her bike, strapping her feet to the pedals and pushing the bike forward, urging her to push alternately on her left, then right foot in some semblance of rhythm. But even with the training wheels, the foot straps, the pedaling exercises and the helping hands, bicycling proved too ambitious a project for Karen. We couldn't afford to give it a full-time effort—not with school plus her IAHP program and after-school reading and writing practice—so Karen settled for being pushed around on her bike every so often. The bike was put in a corner of the playroom, a shiny goal to be pursued at some later date, and to be loaned to sister Gretchen if she behaved herself.

The encouraging thing about Karen's disappointments and handicaps was her attitude toward them. "Tell them the whole thing!" Karen would insist if we had visitors who wondered about Karen's problems and asked a question or two about the progress she had made.

A happy example of Karen's ability to compensate for handicaps was her enthusiastic participation in our Sunday night "shows."

The hour after Sunday evening supper at Eastleigh very often is, at the girls' request, set aside for a "show." The large green bathroom rug is placed before the overstuffed yellow chair, and it is understood by one and all that this rug is the "stage," that the crouching space behind the yellow chair is "backstage," and that anyone in the living room who is not on stage is "the audience."

Most shows consist of Karen and Gretchen reciting school-learned songs and poems, with Karen acting as mistress of ceremonies-announcer, and Barbara or myself shushing John as he groans that the performance is bound to get better before it gets worse. One evening early in 1972, however, the girls earned some genuine applause from John. Daddy the frustrated playwright had composed a Karen-and-Gretchen-sized drama concerning a doll that had been rendered speechless by an evil witch. After John's enthusiastic bravos had subsided, I asked Karen if she wouldn't like to be in the audience the next time, and let John come up on the stage. She shook her head and said no, she would prefer to act.

"Why, Karen?"

"Because I can't make a clapping noise with my hands like the others."

That positive kind of compensation—serving as emcee and performer because Lefty wouldn't let her make a loud clapping noise—is one of Karen's great assets. She will accept a limitation if she must, but is determined to make the most of those abilities she does have.

The spring of 1972 was good to us. Miss Edney told Karen one day that her handwriting was "better than ever," after Karen had written, during the "news" period in class, "we had guests for dinner." John outperformed his Bermudian classmates at their own games by winning the class prize for the cricket ball throw and for making the best Bermuda three-stick kite. And Gretchen proved the best Easter egg decorator in her class.

At our spring visit to The Institutes, we were directed to assemble yet another device to stimulate Karen's vision. "A wall of lights," Glenn Doman called it—five rows of Christmas-tree lights spaced two feet apart, covering an entire wall of our playroom and operated with a control panel so that we could turn the lights on individually or in sequence. The objective was to help Karen scan a scene in an orderly, logical way, and thus be able to "find" an object more rapidly and focus on it, and to interpret the landscape ahead of her more confidently. If it worked, she should, for one thing, be able to walk with less hesitancy.

An American friend and neighbor who worked as a U. S. Navy electronics expert scrounged enough used or obsolete parts to build our control box, and soon after the great blinking wall was completed Karen had caught on very well indeed. She occasionally confused the white and yellow bulbs, but she per-

formed the various games we invented—most of them carried out
while she swung upside down—with increasing speed and confidence.

I suppose the incentive of jelly beans and chocolate eggs had
something to do with it, but in any case we observed a slightly
improved scanning ability on Easter morning when Karen
searched the upstairs rooms for treats the Easter rabbit had left
in her name. She still had difficulty finding objects that blended
in with the background, but she was making a better effort to
scan and was better able to follow our verbal clues. Perhaps, we
decided, Easter egg hunting ought to be a regular part of her
program.

As Karen's walking confidence increased, we became more and
more aware that her arms went automatically into the primary
balance position—bent at the elbow and slightly outstretched—
every time she got onto her feet. She could "think" her arms
down, but as soon as she would turn her mind to other matters,
her forearms rose reflexively. Barbara tried giving her weighted
objects to hold, but she would either drop them or lift them up
to the primary balance position.

One day after school she produced a couple of stick figures
with arms that reached their feet and I asked, when I got
home, "Why are the arms so long, Karen?"

"I'm pretending I walk with my arms down," she replied. "I
made them nearly down to my feet, so they have to stay down."

One April day, Karen arrived home from school with the report, "We had a new girl in our class today. Her name's Roberta.
Isn't that good news?"

Continuing with the "good news," she reported that Roberta
had asked, "Why do you walk that way?"—and that she had replied easily, "Because I was sick when I was two."

Karen had fielded that question so well—I should have known
better than to offer any advice on the matter. But I thought a
few words on the subject of empathy might be in order and
might help Karen make a new friend.

"You must be friendly to Roberta," I said. "It's not easy coming to a new school in the middle of the year and not knowing any of the other children."

Her response was slightly condescending. "Oh Daddy," she said, "we're already friends."

Karen wasn't able to join in many of the joyous jump-up-and-down games that six- and seven-year-old girls like to play, and her IAHP program hadn't left time for her share of give-and-take experiences with other little girls. Yet she had learned the basic lesson of friendship—that to have friends you must be a friend—and that was saying a great deal for a little girl who for a very large part of her young life had been pretty much out of touch with the world of childhood.

She said one spring evening, as I was helping her make her way up the stairs from the playroom, that it certainly would be nice "when I don't need help for anything." Yet her dependency had had its brighter side: Because she had always been appreciative of help (when needed), people had enjoyed helping her. She had been touched by love, and she in turn loved "everybody"—and the world was a bit better for it.

In the first week of May 1972, Karen received five birthday party invitations—three from youngsters she had not invited to her party. One Lyne, two Sharons, a Chuck and a Marc. Everyone but Gretchen, who had received more invitations over a period of a year but had only been invited to accompany Karen to two of the five current parties, rejoiced with Karen.

On May 25 Barbara and Karen had an appointment at The Institutes, and for the first time Karen was not at all anxious to go. It wasn't all the probing, questioning, waiting, and demonstrating she objected to; what really bothered her was that being in Philadelphia on May 25 meant she would be obliged to miss her first Sports Day at Somerset Primary.

Sports Day, an annual event at all Bermuda schools, had been the subject of excited discussion in our home and in school. On the eve of our first Sports Day, three years earlier, brother John, who has more than his share of athletic ability, had been quaking in his gym shoes. He developed an unlikely collection of pains and palpitations, apparently because he feared humiliation on the field of battle. But he had come home from that first Sports Day with two ribbons and had been a Sports Day enthusiast ever since. Now Karen's and Gretchen's first date with Sports Day was approaching, and they had been looking forward to it.

We had assumed that Karen wanted to be a spectator, to be on hand when her friends competed against others in the school. But we were wrong.

"I want to race," Karen said.

Even when she was walking, Karen lost her balance often and fell to her knees. And her version of "running" was a bounding sort of motion, more noteworthy for its exuberance than its effectiveness in covering a lot of ground in a hurry. Gretchen was well aware of this, so she declared, hoping to convince her sister that missing the Sports Day races would not be the end of the world, "You couldn't win anything anyway, Karen."

Karen's response spoke volumes about her.

"I don't care," she said. "I just wanted to be in the race."

CHAPTER XVI
Making It

Sports Day 1972.

John Breisky brought home four ribbons—first in cricket ball throw and long jump, second in the fifty-meter run, third in high-jump—to place second among all the "10 and under" boys at Somerset Primary.

Gretchen won three yellow ribbons, but she was a bit vague as to what they were for. One was for "plain running," one for an egg-and-spoon race, the third for what must have been a sort of romper-set decathlon featuring a sack race and an assortment of obstacles.

And Karen, who had "wanted to race," flew to Philadelphia for her nineteenth revisit to The Institutes for the Achievement of Human Potential.

Sandy Brown took Karen's history on that visit, noting that her neurological and developmental growth rates were excellent, except for the fact that her chest wasn't expanding quite as fast as it should. Then, when Sandy heard of Karen's disappointment at missing Sports Day and of the birthday invitations from Lyne, Sharon, Sharon, Marc and Chuck, she broke into a triumphant grin and picked up her phone to dial the director's office.

"Listen to this," she began, and proceeded to recite Karen's good news, which, she said, was too urgent to be circulated via the standard report form.

By the time she hung up, Sandy's grin had mellowed into a

warm smile. "Karen," she declared, enjoying her fair share of the triumph, "has made it."

And Karen had, of course. Karen had served notice that she would be heard from. She had won the respect of doubters because of the skills she had developed, the respect of our friends by the determination she had demonstrated, and finally, the respect of Miss Edney's class for both these reasons and for the friendship she had offered so freely. She had "made it" not because her problems had evaporated, but because she had got her feet stuck in what poet Langston Hughes has called "the sweet flypaper of life."

She had "made it" despite the many lingering problems that resulted from the assault on her brain, precisely five years earlier, and that continued to concern The Institutes staff as well as Barbara and myself. "Midbrain mannerisms" was the IAHP's collective label for most of these problems. Karen was frustrated, too, of course, but she had found healthy ways of venting this frustration, of defeating handicaps with humor, and of probing the flanks when a frontal assault on a problem seemed foolhardy.

Scores of people had joined in the campaign to help Karen "make it," but one of the most effective helpers was a small person whose greatest contribution was simply in serving as a pacesetter: Gretchen.

On the Saturday before we left for Philadelphia, where we were to receive the verdict that Karen had made it, we had a leisurely lunch at Eastleigh, followed by a game of "sums," a mental exercise in simple arithmetic. Gretchen was beating Karen to the answers consistently, and I explained that Gretchen was winning because she had developed the knack of counting on her fingers.

Karen apparently despaired of transmitting, as rapidly as Gretchen, the thousands of brain messages required to achieve finger-counting skill, because she responded, finally, with, "Give us a hard one, Daddy—something Gretchen can't count with her hands."

Earlier that same day, Gretchen had slipped out onto the upstairs porch for an unauthorized ride on Karen's two-wheeler-with-training-wheels and had been gently upbraided by her sister. "You didn't ask if you could ride my bike, Gretchen."

"Here, Karen" was Gretchen's immediate reply. "Let me help you put your slippers on."

Gretchen did have an edge on her older sister in almost any contest demanding a quick response from eyes, hands or feet. But the finger-counting and bike-borrowing incidents illustrated more than that. They illustrated that while Karen's desire to compete was quickening, her defensive mechanisms were in working order, too. She was capable of petulance, but she was also capable of recognizing her limitations without accepting them as permanent or final. She was re-enforcing a self-image that embraced realism and optimism, competitiveness and determination.

Sandy Brown and The Institutes staff have perhaps better perspective than any group of people in the world on the complex process of "making it." Also ranking rather high among those who can perceive when a brain-injured child has made it are IAHP parents, for whom the process of making it usually begins on the first evaluation visit, and never really ends. You soon observe that what seems an overwhelming handicap to one child may seem a mere inconvenience to another. Certainly positive attitudes—the attitudes of both parent and youngster—often play a significant role. For many, however, a single problem or a crushing combination of problems can conspire to defeat even the most positive or noble of attitudes.

We remember a hyperactive Puerto Rican boy who was well on his way to making it. For the first ten years of his life he had not been able to walk, despite the best neurological and physical-therapy advice his well-to-do parents could find in Puerto Rico and in New York. We met him in Philadelphia after he had been on the IAHP program for a mere three months, and he was loping up and down the halls. There was no containing him.

We suspect that Boris made it, too. Boris was a Yugoslav-

Italian child who lived in Italy. We saw him only once, at The Institutes, but still vividly recall his jubilant and engaging spirit, which so well reflected that of his parents. Boris was creeping on hands and knees when we met, and Karen was still perfecting her tummy-crawling. Boris spoke only Italian and Karen only English, yet they were kindred spirits—determined, effervescent. *"Mascarina!"* Boris shouted with delight when he observed us fitting Karen's rebreathing mask on her face. It was the first time he had seen anyone but himself wearing such a mask.

We remember the boy who set his own timer for patterning, and the Michigan youngster who was just learning to talk at age four and a half, but could read, and we suspect that they have made it.

We wonder from time to time about Edmund, moderately brain-injured at birth and never really shunted onto the right track. We met him at a Sunday school, where he seemed happy—yet shortly thereafter his parents withdrew him. "Edmund loves everybody," his mother told us somewhat bitterly, "but not everyone loves Edmund."

I made a point not long ago of finding out how Timmy was getting on. Timmy was the ten-year-old Enfield boy who had been sporting enough to put down his beloved bike and come inside to give us a patterning demonstration when we were trying to get Karen going on a program but had not yet been able to get an appointment at The Institutes. On a business trip from Bermuda to New York in late 1972 I tracked down Timmy's parents. Timmy had been enrolled at The Institutes at age nine, "in hopes," his father said, "that he could attain normal intelligence." They had quit after eighteen months because he seemed to have made no real improvement—beyond the fact that he had begun to sing. He had, in fact, developed epilepsy, and his parents couldn't help harboring the feeling that patterning might have "set it off." (Seizures are a common symptom of brain injury—Karen had had terrifying ones in the hospital—and there is always the possibility that they can occur. But they rarely develop while a child is on the program, says the IAHP. A staff member once told us that while taking a history during one youngster's initial visit, the mother reported that her child had begun having seizures for the first time just a few days earlier. The mother went on to say that if the seizures had commenced two weeks later, after the child was on the program, she would have been convinced the program had *caused* them.)

I also checked back on the supermarket owner's teen-aged daughter we had heard of—a youngster who could walk and read but hadn't been able to run or ride a bike. Her parents had enrolled her at The Institutes in hopes that her mobility might improve, but they, too, had been disappointed in the results. She's a young woman now and is having "some psychological problems," because her former school friends have gone their separate ways and she feels abandoned. Her father was down on the Doman-Delacato methods when last I spoke to him.

"Making it" is for many a state of mind. I suppose no one who has suffered massive, diffuse brain injury can ever entirely recover all the function that was lost. But sheer determination helps many stalwart spirits make it despite severe disabilities.

Certainly age has some bearing on a youngster's chances of making it. Brain maturation is nearly complete when a child starts school, and the more years of growth the brain has ahead, after it has been injured, the better. That might help explain the disenchantment of the two Enfield families we had known; they had gone on the program when their children were nine and thirteen respectively. But what of Sue Lynn Carroll, who seemed to have suffered precisely the same loss of function as Karen, at the same age and in the same way? Sue Lynn's parents, Ed and Joanne, had if anything made a more determined effort than we to help their daughter make the grade. It had seemed as if every available pair of arms in the Carrolls' high-rise apartment building in the Riverdale section of the Bronx had been mobilized in Sue Lynn's behalf. Moreover, Joanne's twenty-three-year-old sister had given up her job for two full years—despite Joanne's protests that "you have your own life to lead"—in an effort somehow to start the wheels of progress rolling for her niece.

Yet Sue Lynn has not yet, except perhaps in a spiritual sense, begun to make it. She simply didn't respond to the IAHP's best efforts—even a last-ditch "coma program," wherein her senses of taste, smell, feeling and hearing were assaulted throughout her waking hours.

Sue Lynn is off The Institutes program now, still unable to see, speak, or move her body in any meaningful way. Like playwright Peter Nichols's little girl, she must be sedated regularly to forestall seizures. The sedation curbs her alertness and makes her less responsive to stimulation, and thus she seems trapped within a conspiracy of interwining impediments. She is put in her custom-made wheelchair every morning and taken aboard a bus for a trip to a physical therapy center in the city. A "holding action," her parents call this present program—a means of keeping her limber and allowing her mother time for Sue Lynn's two younger sisters, while Ed and Joanne seek word of a breakthrough or some other form of miracle.

Boris of the *mascarina*, Ed and Joanne Carroll's sleeping beauty, Timmy the bike rider, and the Puerto Rican boy who discovered walking at the age of ten—these youngsters and others had given us the perspective to know what Sandy Brown meant when she declared that "Karen has made it."

In the weeks that followed, back in Bermuda, Karen continued taking more small steps toward the increased independence she would need in order to cope with the world. I would find laboriously chalked messages—such as "Daddy take us to the dolphin show"—scrawled on the playroom slate when I returned from work in the evening. And Karen surprised everyone by descending the outside steps without help—on her bottom, one step at a time—after Gretchen and a young visitor had abandoned her on the upper yard.

During the final week of Karen's first year as a schoolgirl, we had a cookout on the porch. The steak caught fire and Karen threatened, "You know what I'm going to tell for my news in school tomorrow? 'We had dinner on the porch. We had potatoes and bread and charcoal.'"

That "news" was duly reported, and on Karen's final report card of the year Miss Edney noted: "Karen has tried hard and attempted everything the class has done with very little assistance from myself. She is making progress. She is a lively and interested member of the class."

We celebrated that progress, a month later, by indulging ourselves in what would be Karen's first sabbatical from "the program"—a farm vacation in Britain, first on a sheep farm among the lochs and heather of Perthshire, which Sir Walter Scott, an Edinburgh man, had called "the fairest portion of the northern kingdom," and later on a dairy farm in Devon, on the fringe of mist-shrouded Dartmoor.

Our headquarters in Perthshire was Crosshead Farm, some two hundred rolling acres just east of the town of Crieff, gateway to the lower highlands. Crosshead was given over primarily to sheep and barley and was operated by Mr. and Mrs. John Gow. Our rooms there had been arranged by Alastair Morrison, who not long after H.M.S. *Mohawk* exercises in Bermuda waters had completed his tour of duty with the Royal Navy and had taken unto him a bonnie bride named Margaret.

En route to Crieff we flew into Edinburgh, feasted on strawberries, walked the Royal Mile through a fine mist, outfitted the kids in Wellingtons and slickers, and willingly paid our landlady an additional ten pence for a bath to rinse off the dust from the trip and five pence for enough amps to ignite our bedside reading lamp and plan our drive to Perthshire.

Alastair and Margaret met us outside Edinburgh at the village of Loanhead, where we had a gala reunion with Alastair's shipmate Ronnie Douglas, and with Ronnie's Kathleen and their wee bairn, Leah.

Our timing for visiting Perthshire was good. The sheep-shearing and the haying had been finished at Crosshead, and the harvesting was still a few weeks away, so Mrs. Gow was able to take guests in the two front rooms and show little children how to prepare a milk bottle for a pet lamb named Dixie.

There were chores for the children: John worked in the cow barn; Lefty and Righty were assigned to help with the egg-cleaning by Mrs. Gow, who perceived immediately how pleased Karen would be to be singled out for such a delicate task; and Gretchen sketched Bermuda scenes to decorate the "drying room," where Mr. Gow and his farmhands hung their coats before the fire and drank mugs of tea.

And there were half-day excursions: to the Castle of Doune, home of the Stuart Clan in the perilous times of the later Middle Ages; to the heather-hued hills of the Sma' Glen, scene of the Gathering of the Clans as they armed for the Jacobite Rising in 1715, and where sheep and highland cattle now range; with a farmhand named Gordon to a remote and roiling stream near Lednoch, where fish refused to rise to my flies but where John, casting with worms, landed three brown trout for his and Mr. Gow's breakfast; and to Lochearnhead, for bell heather and foxglove to be pressed into the children's scrapbooks.

Down Hill Street, Crieff, past the Temperance Hotel and the fish-'n'-chips shop the children marched, on the heels of the Strathearn Pipe Band as it headed, Pied Piper-like, for a "highland night" performance. And when Barbara and I had an evening out with Alastair and Margaret, with dinner along the River Earn at Comrie and then a folk concert with the laird of the land himself handling the lights, it was Mrs. Gow who told the bedtime tales and tucked in our bra' band. (Mr. Gow, in a Sunday suit, had been out the door ahead of us. "He's away to the bowling—that's where that man goes," Mrs. Gow explained. "And *leaves* his wife. He's bowling-daft and curling-daft, that man is.")

From our farm in Perthshire, in central Scotland, we moved to a seventeenth-century thatch-roofed manor farmhouse in southwest England—East Ash Manor, which is near the crossroads village of Throwleigh, within the Dartmoor National Park and a mile from the edge of the moor itself.

East Ash Manor, operated by Charles and Veronica Mosse, featured two cream labradors (Honey and Bess), three ponies (Teasel, Peso and Butterscotch), three children (Anne, David and Rosalind), seventy-five unnamed dairy cows, numerous pigs, chickens and barnswallows, an occasional fox or badger, a vast country kitchen where a superb farm-fresh dinner for sixteen was served nightly, and a downstairs playroom with toys for the children and a mantelpiece lined with books relating the lore and legend of the moors.

The pirates', smugglers', and fishermen's ports of Devon and Cornwall were temptingly near, but we decided to limit our explorations to the tiny inland villages nearest the farm—Throwleigh, Gidleigh, Whiddon Down, Chagford—to the maze of hedgerows and narrow lanes connecting the villages, and to the moors themselves. Less is more, says the architect Mies van der Rohe, and we found that this dictum applied to outings with Karen as well as to contemporary architecture. The less we tried to see and do—the more time we gave Karen to focus her eyes and get her bearings—the more she was able to comprehend and the more we all were able to enjoy.

One day we set out in search of "the rheumatism stone," at one of the dolmens, or prehistoric communal burial places, erected on the moors by Neolithic man, so they say. We failed to find the dolmen we sought, but did come upon a reasonable facsimile, and passed Karen through the opening, just in case it possessed the curative powers attributed to the rheumatism stone.

The best hours were spent hiking, out of sight of all traces of modern man, among the wild Dartmoor ponies—many with foal—where John and Gretchen ran free and Karen became increasingly surefooted on the lumpiest terrain she had ever encountered.

"That was a great day," Karen would say as we made our way back to the farm.

There was donkey-riding for the kids at the Throwleigh Fayre, and cantering across the moors on a pony trek for Barbara and me, and "Somerset clotted cream served at the intervals" during an outdoor performance of *The Fantastiks,* and lunching at the Tinners' Rabbits in Chagford while we wondered what life was like here in the early fourteenth century when the village was established for the assaying and taxing of tin mined from the surrounding moorland.

Before we knew it, there was a train to catch—the girls' first train ride—from Exeter in to London's Paddington Station, and London tubes and double-decker buses to experience, and a chimpanzee's tea party to see at the London Zoo, and the Rupert Bear Show to endure.

We returned home happy and invigorated. The trip had expanded Karen's visual horizons, enabling her to store away visual images of castles and sheep, bagpipes and heather—and if that wasn't rationale enough, the trip had been worthwhile just for the opportunity of abandoning "the program" and our other daily responsibilities for three weeks.

Karen returned to her IAHP-orchestrated program as if she hadn't missed a beat, welcoming her overhead ladder as a long-lost friend, reading seven pages in her *Happy Venture Reader* on her first full day at home, climbing our stairs for the first time without an assisting hand, and also for the first time removing her pants and sock (left).

We had been home for less than two weeks when Karen, Barbara and I received an invitation to take yet another trip. Every second year, two of the IAHP youngsters who have "made it" are invited to appear with their parents before an assemblage of men who play a large role in supporting The Institutes' work—the convention of the United Steelworkers of America. The 1972 convention was to be held in the gambling mecca of Las Vegas, which we had never seen and had never intended to see. Yet on reflection it seemed an appropriate place for the official celebration of Karen's five-year miracle. We had, after all, been told by a Hartford brain doctor before we applied to The Institutes that we would be gambling a fairly large chunk of money if we went there, and that the odds were very poor indeed.

CHAPTER XVII

Taking Part

"It seems to be one of those things that man is challenged by," said the lean, angular, balding young man at the microphone, "to always go further, to climb higher and learn more. That is inherent in human nature. You have it; we all have it."

He had not yet met Karen, for he had preceded her on the agenda, yet when Apollo XVI astronaut Thomas K. Mattingly spoke as he did on man's will to achieve, in the course of his address to the more than eight thousand union delegates assembled in the Las Vegas Convention Center, it seemed he was talking directly to Karen.

Seated on the platform of the sixteenth Constitutional Convention of the United Steelworkers of America were three long rows of union officials, politicians and assorted guests. Among the guests were two young ladies who had flown with their parents from Somerset, Bermuda, and Scranton, Pennsylvania, to demonstrate to the steelworkers the sort of miracle that their union's sustaining contribution to The Institutes could help bring about. (The steelworkers' money has been vitally important to The Institutes since 1968, when virtually all the IAHP's foundation support was cut off following a medical journal article that claimed the Doman-Delacato methods were "unproved.")

Waiting their turn to step up to the microphone, Glenn Doman, Abbe Heller and Karen Breisky set up a "hugs and kisses factory" on the platform. ("The hugs go in the red box," The Institutes director explained, "and the kisses in the green box.")

There was talk from the speaker's platform of how a "Ban the Can" campaign—a recycling effort urged by environmentalists—might threaten steelworkers' jobs. Delegates named Piontek, Harding and Guagliardo stood at microphones placed at what seemed quarter-mile intervals in the mammoth hall and sought recognition to have their say on strike funds, grievances and arbitration.

Then Glenn Doman was introduced. He spoke briefly of the application of The Institutes' theories to well children around the world—how three-year-olds were being taught to play the violin by the Japanese, and to ride horseback by the Sioux, and how newborn babies were being taught to swim in Australia— and how people involved in these programs were converging on The Institutes to obtain neurological answers as to how these and other skills are possible for young children.

"A little girl who started out to be part of the world's problem but who is going to be part of the world's answer" was the way Glenn Doman chose to introduce ten-year-old Abbe Heller—who had been blue at birth, a preemie, totally limp. When Abbe reached her first birthday, he said, a panel of medical school professors had predicted she would never develop beyond a mental age of ten or twelve years—yet by nineteen months of age she could read thirty words, and when she stepped up onto the stage of the steelworkers' convention, she was a bright, ten-year-old fifth-grader who required a back brace and high-powered corrective lenses, but enjoyed dancing, swimming and handicrafts and had just written a little speech which she declined to show to anyone until the morning of the day she was to deliver it.

"I'd like you to meet Abbe Heller," said Glenn Doman.

"Hi," said Abbe to the convention.

"Go ahead," the IAHP director urged her.

"Thank you for the wonderful time in Las Vegas."

"Do you want to say anything else?"

"My mother and my father and me are having a great time."

"Do you want to say anything else?"

"Because if it wasn't for the clinic, I wouldn't be on this stage today and I wouldn't be walking, talking, reading and writing and going to school, and maybe I wouldn't even be alive today. So thank you very much for being so very kind to me."

Standing ovation from eight thousand steelworkers.

And then it was the turn of Karen Breisky, three years and six inches Abbe's junior but no more awed by her surroundings than Abbe had been.

"Karen was blind, blind, blind," Glenn Doman said after capsulizing her five-year struggle. "As blind as it's possible to be. She was paralyzed and limp. That day began five years of extremely hard work. Five years have gone by, and Karen is still on the program, but Karen is no longer paralyzed. While it is still not perfect, Karen walks. Believe it or not, Karen is no longer blind, and now reads not with her fingers but with her eyes. Karen, like Abbe, is on her way. Not to averageness, but to superiority.

"I would like to tell you a story about Karen," he said—and the story he had in store was our Sports Day story.

"*I want to race.*"

"*You won't be missing anything, Karen. You couldn't win anything, anyway.*"

"*I don't care. I just wanted to be in the race.*"

Institutes director Doman related that when he and his wife were in England shortly after hearing the Sports Day story, they saw what they felt would be a singularly appropriate trophy to present to Karen in Las Vegas—a Wedgwood commemorative plate with a raised figure of a runner at the center. "Olympiad XX Munich 1972" was inscribed in gold letters at the bottom, and at the top was a paraphrasing of Karen's Sports Day retort —"Not The Winning But The Taking Part."

Barbara and I swallowed very hard as Karen was lifted to the mike to say something to an assemblage of delegates who had already heard from the governor of Nevada, the U. S. Secretary of Labor, an Apollo XVI astronaut, Steelworkers president I. W. Abel, IAHP director Glen Doman, and Abbe Heller.

Grinning happily, Karen took a deep breath and shouted at the microphone, "Hello, Steelworkers!"

That was all she said, all she had to say, all she had a chance to say, before her standing ovation.

Karen was a queen for three days and three nights in Las Vegas. She gaped at the trapeze artists and cycling poodles at the Circus Circus casino and was forgiven for snoring softly during Count Basie and Tony Bennett's joint rendition of "Don't Get Around Much Anymore." Room service at the Las Vegas Hilton was at her beck and call, courtesy of her friends the steelworkers, and she decided the Creamed Chicken on Toast Points and the Internationale Fresh Fruit Salad with Sherbet sounded very nice.

In mid-October 1972, a month after Las Vegas, Karen was asked by her father if she would object to his converting the notebooks known as "my book" into a real book, and she thought that would be great.

I wanted to produce a printed record that would serve as a permanent reminder to Karen, and to the rest of the world, that at age seven our eldest daughter had already achieved more than most humans are called upon to achieve in a lifetime. (The IAHP, moreover, now gave its blessing to a book about Karen. Their onetime concern about a depressingly long waiting list, and the knowledge that favorable publicity served to make the list even longer, had lessened as more and more of The Institutes program was being adopted by other rehabilitation centers—and, unhappily, since the medical journal article that challenged IAHP theories as "unproved.")

The recognition, in the Las Vegas Convention Center, of Karen's Olympic spirit seemed when I began writing Karen's story to be the obvious stopping point for her book. The best chapters of her life should be ahead of her, but every book must have a final chapter, and the vast stage of the Las Vegas Convention Center seemed an appropriate, if unlikely, place to say, "The End."

At this present point in time, after eight months of book-writing—eight more months of watching Karen "taking part"—

that elevated stage in Las Vegas still seems a good vantage point for Karen's curtain call. Except that what is past is prologue, and what has happened over these past eight months seems to offer a few more clues as to some of the things Karen can expect to look forward to.

I. *Karen will continue to progress, by degrees.*

Among the first in her class to learn to tell time accurately this year was Karen Breisky—because Karen had applied herself to an informal course in time-telling at home, with a clock-face game and a foot-wide cardboard clock dial as training aids.

After nearly five years of "masking" Karen as often as eighteen times a day, we were told we might retire our rebreathing masks along with other relics from Karen's age of helplessness. Karen was decreed active enough to get all the lung-filling, deep-breathing opportunities she needed, now that she had progressed to a basic form of running and jumping. (*Running:* In the spring of '72 she could run from kitchen to living room, via John's room, and back to kitchen again in 38.5 seconds. By the spring of '73 she had reduced her time to 21 seconds. Gretchen, meanwhile, had been clocked at 8.5. But "taking part" doesn't mean beating Gretchen; it means being willing to join Gretchen in the competition, and competing against your own past record. *Jumping:* At 7:15 P.M. on Monday, May 6, 1973, Karen skipped rope. A single skip— nothing more than lifting both feet off the ground, once, as Barbara and I swung a skipping rope over her head and commanded, "Jump!" But a splendid achievement, a fine moment.)

Latest record for undressing herself at bedtime: removing an unbuttoned cardigan sweater, elastic-waisted slacks, underpants, both shoes and both socks.

March 28, 1973: best-yet demonstration of clapping. Karen decided she may, after all, be able to take a leave of absence from the stage and join the audience during our Sunday night "show."

Gretchen is demonstrating her ability to outpace Karen in both reading and writing skills on any time-clock test. But Karen the listener maintains her lead in vocabulary and remains number one at recognizing words spelled out verbally rather than on paper. (It was after-dinner-coffee time, and a broad hint that I didn't seem to have a spoon had made no apparent impression on Barbara. "Boy," I said at last, spelling out a key word, "the service really s-t-i-n-k-s around here." Instantly and gleefully, Karen cried out, "Stinks!")

Visual progress? Assuredly yes, but the evidence is contradictory and often seems to defy analysis. Pointing to a Bermuda chimney similar to one on a Christmas scene we had shown her months earlier, Karen announced recently to Barbara, "That's the kind of chimney Santa can't get down." When a pair of fourteen-year-old identical twins visited us earlier in the year, Karen stated flatly, "They can't be twins—Paul is wearing black sneakers and Mark is wearing white." And looking across the Great Sound at night, at the strings of red and white lights, she declared, "I can see everything across the water—*everything!*" Yet when Barbara took Karen to the Gesell Institute of Child Development in New Haven recently for an evaluation by an optometrist whose work parallels that of The Institutes in many respects, she was thought to be "visually lost" in strange surroundings. (The optometrist was optimistic, however. He prescribed bifocals, with portions of each lens blacked out by tape, and an intriguing new series of exercises.)

Visually lost? Once upon a time there was a sightless little girl named Karen who could identify things and people only by touch, or by the sounds they made, but she wasn't altogether "lost" even then. One day she sat in the office of Sandra Brown at The Institutes and an object was placed in her left hand. No response. But as her Lefty succeeded in passing the object to her Righty, which was far more discerning, the little girl said with a flash of recognition, *"Now* I see it."

II. *Karen and family will experience our fair share of hurts and joys.*

A visitor to my office was making a crude attempt at humor.

"That twit!" he said. "The man's a regular spastic." As if
spasticity were a cause for shame, a measure of ignorance.

In preparation for a party at Somerset Primary, each of the
Infant School youngsters had been required to fashion a party
hat of crepe paper and to decorate it. Gretchen's was gay and
imaginative, but she pouted, "Lorianne copied mine." Karen,
whose hat was considerably less artistic than Gretchen's, was
characteristically buoyant: "Nobody copied mine!" We pointed
out to Gretchen, but not to Karen, that imitation is the greatest
form of flattery.

"Real running" in the schoolyard is joy unrestrained. But
there's a price to pay—a pair of knees battered by almost daily
spills. (Karen has been learning to fall with a bit more dignity,
however. She and Gretchen were in our bedroom one winter's
morning, conspiring over how they could obtain a chum's phone
number so that they might call her. I must have startled Karen
as I entered the room, for she lost her balance and fell to her
knees—but regained her composure in an instant, declaring, "I
thought maybe if I got down and did a couple of tricks for you,
you would help us call Sharon.")

On their springtime 1973 visit to The Institutes, Karen and
Barbara stayed as usual with Sally and Ralph Streibig just outside Philadelphia. On the morning after her evaluation Karen
was invited to join in a neighborhood Easter egg hunt, and she
could hardly contain herself. Her eyes and legs did their very
best, and that was almost good enough. At the signal, she ran
toward an egg she had spied, became slightly outraged when
another youngster reached it ahead of her, and overlooked two
more eggs that were virtually at her feet. Then suddenly she
ran off by herself, her paper bag clutched by Lefty, melting into
the crowd of scurrying kids, hardly noticeable. Total yield: five
eggs, all chocolate. Eight-year-old Erich Streibig had collected
about twenty. Karen seemed unhappy at first because she had
so few, so Barbara asked her to stand still and listen while the
other children reported their hauls to their mothers. Karen
brightened considerably when she heard, "I got three!" and "I

didn't find *any*" and when four-year-old Gregg Streibig (who only answers to "Daffy Duck") finally returned from his hunt and reported that he had had only two until a lady took pity and slipped a few into his basket.

A few conclusions on the subject of hurts and joys: While Karen will have her share of hurts to go along with the joys, and setbacks along with accomplishments, these hurts and setbacks are likely to be minimized because she has a caring and intelligent mother to work with her, and because her parents have the wherewithal to take her to Philadelphia and to take on a summer helper to assist with "the program," and because I was fortunate enough to land a job in Bermuda, where the climate is gentle and the stress is less and where Karen was not obliged to be isolated from "normal" school as a result of her limitations.

All these factors matter a great deal. Every article I've seen and clipped since May of 1967 on the subject of brain injury points to the significance of certain more or less self-evident truths: that child-rearing practices play a large role in determining whether a child born with even minor brain dysfunction will overcome his problems or become a failure in school; that brain-injured kids born to families in the "upper socioeconomic strata" stand a better chance; that the sooner a brain-injured child receives help (from someone who knows what he's talking about), the better his chances of success; that proper diet—rich in proteins, well-balanced nutritionally—can make a significant difference; that children with neurologic learning disabilities (and that could mean a mobility problem, a depth-perception problem, a memory-storing problem, a hyperactivity problem) will do better work if not isolated from other "normal" ("average," the IAHP would say) children.

In all these respects, good fortune has been on Karen's side. God only knows how many tens of thousands of children there are whose brain injury has been *caused* by protein deficiency; whose symptoms their mothers are unable or unwilling to see, much less overcome; who have been tucked away in asylums because their emotional disturbances were allowed to camouflage the real source of their problem(s).

III. *Karen's tomorrows will be full of surprises. She will be touched, shaped, influenced, by events, things, places and people we cannot conceive of today.*

A grapefruit-sized rubber ball on a string was prescribed for Karen by the Gesell Institute. We were instructed to put her on her back on the floor and suspend the ball over her, moving it back and forth slowly, as a signal for her to open and close her arms and legs in unison. We were also to swing the ball to her while she was standing, and let her practice catching it and socking it with a lightweight bat. Gretchen offered to help with all of this, assuring us she could handle the job very nicely— then proceeded to knock out one of Karen's baby teeth with one of her first swings of the ball. The world is booby-trapped in ingenious ways.

En route from Scotland to Devon last summer, we stayed in the tiny village of Axbridge, just south of Bristol. We bought stamps and postcards in the village's combination post office and stationery shop, and a *Times* and *Telegraph* from the news agent, strolled through the old square where butchers once were treated to drinks by the town fathers when they tendered the quarterly rent payments for their stalls, aimed a movie camera at a bicycling postman as he delivered the morning mail to the butcher shop. Eight months later we read that sixty-three members of the Axbridge Ladies' Guild had gathered in the village square to board a bus for Bristol airport, and less than two hours later had crashed into a snowy slope in Switzerland. The postman's wife was lost, and the news agent's wife, and the butcher's wife, and many, many others. Forty-seven Axbridge children lost their mothers that day, in that village of twelve hundred. "Axbridge will never be the same," the Ladies' Guild chairman told one reporter. "Not in my generation and not in the next. Never." We had stayed in a tenth-century fortress town which had seemed somehow changeless—and then, "it will never be the same."

"You change and change and change, outstripping these words even as I set them down," wrote Paul West to his daughter Mandy in his perceptive book, *Words for a Deaf Daughter*.

And so it is with Karen, and with all of us. We cannot forecast tomorrow; neither can we pretend that our use, or waste, of today will make no difference.

IV. *The cast of characters in "Karen's World" will continue to grow. Unlikely newcomers will make unexpected appearances, while some of those in key supporting roles will depart the scene.*

The cast of "Karen's World" grew by at least a dozen on a Sunday morning a few months back, when we lost Karen's doll in Newark Airport and a task force of airport employees suddenly mobilized itself to form a search party. The doll was returned unharmed.

The cast was diminished by one very central character in the first month of 1973 when even a pacemaker proved inadequate to the task of stimulating the heartbeat of our beloved Nana Liz. Confronted for the first time with the death of a member of the family, our children asked the difficult questions about the human spirit, or soul. "We would like to think," I told them, "that Nana Liz is already with God in heaven."

Karen couldn't quite accept that. "I'd like to think," she said, "that Nana Liz was still here with us."

The cast was enriched in March of 1973 when Gail Mann brought her fifteen-month-old son Steven to Eastleigh for a visit shortly after a diagnosis of brain injury had been confirmed by a pediatric neurologist in Montreal. Käthe Kirchmeier was spending her Easter holiday with us at the time, and she and Barbara gave Steven and his mother a patterning demonstration and a crash course in stimulation techniques we had learned. The Manns wrote The Institutes for an appointment and were given a date five months hence, but the achievements Steven

made in the first weeks of attempting the basic procedures
Barbara had demonstrated brought about such an extraordinary
transformation that we almost began to wonder if he would be
needing a trip to Philadelphia. When Steven first came to call
at age fifteen months, he was listless, soundless, content to sit
in one spot by the hour. After two months of intensive stimulation he could have taught a class in creeping. He was pulling
himself into a standing position, "getting into things" in the
best tradition of toddlers, and making the early sounds that
precede speech. Steven has a number of unsolved problems—
such as a wandering eye and an inability to chew his food—
but Steven obviously is going to make it.

Love has made Karen's world go around. Love of God. Love
of Karen. Love of humankind. Love of self, even—self-respect,
if you will—because working with Karen, knowing her, has had
a nourishing effect on many a "self." Love has generated most
of the energy needed to accomplish the task.

Love was very much in evidence just two Sundays ago, when
Sharon Bailey made her departure from Karen's world, and
Bill Brooks became a central character.

Sharon's father had received his orders from the Canadian
Armed Forces, transferring him from Bermuda to western
Canada. On her final day in Somerset Primary, Sharon, aged
seven, had been solemnly advised by Lyne Genereux, aged
seven, "Don't worry, Sharon, I'll sit next to Karen and help her
when she needs it." During Karen and Sharon's final visit
together, on the following Sunday, a cup of lemonade was
spilled on the girls' bedroom floor. (Karen to Barbara: "Mom,
I just want to ask you one thing. Does lemonade make a stain?"
Barbara to Karen: "Okay—where did you spill it?" Karen to
Barbara: "*Mom!* We're cleaning it up!") Karen fished through
her jewelry box for a treasure that would make a suitable farewell gift for her good friend Sharon, and then we drove Sharon
home. I wanted to make Sharon aware of how grateful all of us
were for her steadfast friendship through Karen's first two years

of "real school," but all I could find to say was, "You've been a very big help to Karen, and that has meant a lot to us." To which Sharon replied, "Oh, that's okay. Karen has helped me a lot, too."

Bill Brooks swam into Karen's world on that Sunday, just as Sharon Bailey was saying her good-bys. A short, boundlessly patient man of sixty-three, who since his early teens has spent virtually all of his life within splashing distance of a swimming pool, Bill served as head swimming coach at Harvard for a quarter of a century. Coach Brooks took Bermuda Olympic swimming teams to Berlin in 1936, to London in 1948, and to Helsinki in 1952, and has also spent eighteen summers preaching his remarkable swimming gospel to young Bermudians.

"Chin down. Shoulders under the water. Fish don't swim with their shoulders out of the water, and you can't either." Every now and again Bill Brooks sounds like a college swimming coach, but when he's with small children, his trademarks are patience and respect for each child's individuality.

Bill Brooks joined Karen's world because one springtime afternoon he decided to pay a call on Bermuda's Director of Tourism, concerning a collapsible, Bermuda-inspired swimming pool he had designed so that mothers could teach their two-year-olds to swim. But the director was in conference and the director's secretary said, "Perhaps Mr. Breisky could help you" —and what happened, of course, was that Mr. Brooks wound up helping Mr. Breisky.

I phoned Mr. Brooks a few weeks later to ask, "Have you ever taught handicapped children to swim?"

Yes, he had had considerable success at the Perkins School for the Blind, in Boston. "Good swimmers don't see where they're going, you know. It's a matter of starting out in the right direction."

"What about a child with a mobility problem, who has particular trouble making her left arm and leg behave as they should?"

"The legs aren't important. The kick is only twenty-five per cent of swimming. You can't swim without some sort of arm paddle, but there are strokes—phases of water play—to suit every child."

"Would you have a look at our Karen, to see if you can give us some tips on giving her more skill in the water?"

"I'd love to."

We had expected an evaluation session, and perhaps a demonstration of a few principles. Instead we got a concentrated course in swimming, with Mr. Brooks driving out to Somerset —half the length of Bermuda—at least every second day before he and his wife had to fly back to Massachusetts for the summer.

"Head down, Karen. Chin on the chest. Fingers straight. Stretch your arms until they hurt; get ready to hold your breath until you burst. This game is called Stay Down Forever. Now, let's try to stay down until Mr. Brooks counts to four."

"Let's try seven," said Karen (who previous to Mr. Brooks had been reluctant to try "one").

Seven was easy.

"Could we try ten?" asked Mr. Brooks.

"I could probly do thirteen."

She did twenty.

Karen surfaces—*splurt!*—with a mouthful of water.

"Dear," says Mr. Brooks, "I wouldn't worry about that. You see, you have a very nice smile, and when you smile while you're swimming you swallow a little water."

Karen is tense. How can Mr. Brooks tell Lefty to relax?

"Oh, there's one other thing. Poor Mr. Brooks—I keep forgetting to tell you things, and this time I forgot to tell you not to hurt my hands. You see, you're squeezing my hands and it hurts."

Report from Karen as we climb the stairs one evening: "Mr. Brooks always says, 'Karen, how do you do it so well?'—and he means it!"

"Here's something new for today," says Mr. Brooks. "We call it the Airplane Float. Now"—arms outstretched—"look at my wings. I want you to try this so you can show Gretchen and John."

Karen makes an attempt, but her "wings" are pointing straight ahead of her. She listens to the critique, and the second time prevails upon Lefty to do his absolute best.

"Karen . . . that one. . . ." Mr. Brooks shakes his head, professing disbelief. "Karen, I'm going to use a new word I've never used before."

"Spell it."

"Spell it? *P—e—r—f—e—c—t*."

"Perfect!"

Well, perhaps not perfect, but Mr. Brooks had made another discovery about Karen, and this time he was exaggerating not at all. Karen had been told by her parents that Mr. Brooks was an AAU medley champion at age fourteen and had coached three Olympic swimming teams—but Mr. Brooks hadn't been told that Karen had stood before eight thousand steelworkers and been presented a trophy that epitomized the spirit of the Olympic Games—"Not The Winning But The Taking Part." So it was all the more meaningful when he lifted her out of the water, sat her on the edge of the pool, and solemnly told her:

"Karen, you're an achiever. That's why you're doing so well. But you're something more than that. You're a winner. You know, there are eight finalists in an Olympic event, and all of them are champions. But when the event is over, there is only one winner. And that's what you are—a winner."

Karen may have greater or more eloquent tributes in store— but that one will serve nicely until a better one comes along.

ROLL OF HONOR

KAREN'S FRIENDS

Karen is what she is—a caring, determined human being who loves "everyone"—to a large extent because of people who helped mold her character with their hands and hearts. "Patterners" we called those who came to assist with her program, but Karen knew them collectively as "my ladies."

Gail Ellis, who began organizing our first brigade of helping hands even before Karen left the hospital, belongs at the head of any such list. To her and to all our very special friends-in-need (a few, we fear, overlooked here), Karen and her family are profoundly grateful.

—W.B.

Hilda and Robin Aitkin
Ethel Assad
Dolly Bean
Marian Berard
Kay Buschlen
Dottie Capece
Fran Carney
Chris and Vince Cavaleri
Maureen and Tim Coleman
Barbara and Bill Cowles
Joe Crowley
Flo and Larry D'Aleo
Mary Jo Descy
Anne DiChiara
Rob Ellis
Dedric Every
Eleanor Finger
Edie Fisher
The Arliss Francises
Eulah Franks

Edna Gamble
Connie Harmon
Bob Hayward
Ann Henry
Mary and Harold Henry
Lou Hitchcock
Gloria Huf
Gwen Barbour Hutchison
Sheila and Diane Kealey
Wilfred Keller
Irene King
The Otto Kirchmeiers
Toni Kweder
Ethel Lambert
Dot Lawrence
Luella Lematta
Stella Lippold
Cynthia Lockwood
Janet McCulloch
Marie, Linda and Maryann

Sally Masters
Bruce Miller
Dorothy Miller and daughters
Kim Morrison
Joan O'Leary
Eileen Outerbridge
Rosemary Outerbridge
Henrietta Palmer
Beatrice Parsons
June Patterson
Joanne Paulsen
Susan Price
Lin Remington
Muriel Roberts
Adela Ruberry

Alice Sawamura
Nancy and Tom Schadlich
Jean Schermerhorn
Gary Simons
Ellerslie Smith
Jean Smith
Olga Smith and sons
Peg Smith
Phyllis Smith
Brenda Tartaglione
Helen Trott
Dianne Uhlinger
Peggy Warwick
Nancy Weatherill
Betty Werther